# of Bertrand Russell

For more than fifty years, in more than one hundred books and articles, Bertrand Russell attacked dogmatic authority as an obstacle to human advancement, with wit, brilliance and lucidity. He gained international eminence as a scientist, philosopher and social critic, and his sometimes unpopular opinions have aroused storms of controversy.

This stimulating and provocative book offers some of his best writings on a wide variety of subjects—psychology, politics, education, religion, ethics and marriage.

Unconventional, outspoken and original, these pieces display Bertrand Russell's genius for exposing the suspicion, fear, lust for power, hatred and intolerance which stand in the way of a better society.

A philosopher who was scientific, yet humane, hopeful and honest, Lord Russell received many honors for his work, including the Order of Merit and the Nobel Prize for Literature.

THIS IS A REPRINT OF THE ORIGINAL HARDCOVER EDITION PUBLISHED BY GEORGE ALLEN AND UNWIN LTD.

BY BERTRAND RUSSELL

BERTRAND RUSSELL'S BEST

Silhouettes in Satire

Selected and Introduced by

Professor Robert E. Egner

New and Revised Centennial Edition

A MENTOR BOOK

NEW AMERICAN LIBRARY

NEW YORK AND SCARBOROUGH, ONTARIO

For Margaret, Chuck, and Dick Egner

Library of Congress Catalog Card Number: 58-12839

Published by arrangement with George Allen & Unwin Ltd.

 MENTOR TRADEMARK REG. U.S. PAT. OFF. AND FOREIGN COUNTRIES
REGISTERED TRADEMARK—MARCA REGISTRADA
HECHO EN WINNIPEG, CANADA

SIGNET, SIGNET CLASSIC, MENTOR, PLUME, MERIDIAN AND NAL BOOKS *are published by New American Library,*
1633 Broadway, New York, New York 10019

12   13   14   15   16   17   18   19   20

PRINTED IN CANADA

Contents

PREFACE BY BERTRAND RUSSELL TO

Bertrand Russell's Best

IT is pleasant news that Professor Egner is publishing a revision of the book *Bertrand Russell's Best*. The skill and the impartiality with which he made his selections, producing, thereby a volume which one may hope can be read without pain and without excessive mental exertion, seem to me admirable. I should like to reiterate, however, what I said in The Preface to the volume edited by Professor Robert E. Egner and Mr Lester E. Denonn called *The Basic Writings of Bertrand Russell*. I said there: 'I should not wish to be thought in earnest only when I am solemn.'

The longer I have lived, the more I have come to suspect solemnity and to see in it—not always, but frequently—a cloak for a humbug. What is most lacking in the modern world is genial, good-natured tolerance; and what is most hostile to this is a harsh and dogmatic morality which condemns the majority of the human race as reprobates. Against solemnity, the best weapon is wit. Most other weapons produce only another dogmatic, sectarian solemnity. I have tried to avoid this danger, though I must confess that I have not always been successful in this endeavour.

Introduction

BERTRAND RUSSELL needs no special introduction to the general reader; his pen was active for almost a century and his more than one hundred books and countless articles travelled a range of thought as wide as the scope of man's quest of knowledge. Lord Russell's position on the great variety of social problems he wrote about was always scientific in the sense that he did not claim pontifical certainty on the views expressed.

Is there a central key to an understanding of the social philosophy of Lord Russell? Is there a certain point at which the general reader, who is not accustomed to philosophical jargon, should begin if he is to read with comprehension and insight? In terms of lucidity, style, and content, the many books and articles from which the material for the present volume was taken amply testify that Lord Russell had no peer among twentieth-century writers. What makes the selections in this book unique, however, is the incisive wit that Lord Russell brought to bear upon such varied subjects as religion, education, ethics, politics, psychology, and sex.

Seldom in history has any major philosopher been able to simultaneously combine intellectual brilliance and humour. Voltaire was the last great wit in philosophical circles, but he was not a mathematician nor a philosopher of any great importance. Although Lord Russell was the victim of extraordinary bigotry during his life, the attacks did not in any way cause him to recant his open views. In this century few thinkers have been more flagrantly misrepresented than Lord Russell. Masses of people have been influenced to envisage him as a mere idol-smasher and the patron philosopher of immorality. It is a false portrait drawn from those twin sins, fear and hate. The fact that he consistently pleaded for benevolence in all spheres of human activity escaped many of his critics. He maintained throughout his life that what the world needed was an old-fashioned thing, an attitude of love or compassion for humanity. Unfortunately his critics passed over his statements to this effect in unrespectful silence.

Lord Russell paid the price for his championship of free thought and inquiry into sexual morality in 1940 in New York when he was declared in court as officially 'unfit' to teach philosophy and logic at the famed City College of New York. The court was implored 'to protect our youth from the baneful influence of him, of the poisoned pen—an ape of genius, the devil's minister to men'. His works were described as sexual filth, but as Lord Russell said, only *one per cent* of his writings were ever concerned with sex in the first place, and he was unfamiliar with filth obtained from scientific inquiry, in the second place. John Dewey seemed to crystallize the views of the intellectual community when he said, 'As Americans we can only blush with shame for this scar on our repute and fair play.' In 1950 a Swedish committee, whose standards are somewhat higher than filth, awarded Lord Russell the Nobel Prize for Literature.

As these pages will show, Lord Russell was mainly concerned with showing how dogmatic authority in its innumerable forms has been, and still remains, one of the great obstacles to human advancement, in terms of an increase in scientific knowledge on the one hand and a decrease in human misery on the other. These selections are funny, but the message beneath the humour is deadly serious. If the reader finds nothing more than surface fun, he is careless and superficial, seeing only the farcical elements before his eyes, and neglecting relations and perspective. One may hold a penny so that it hides the sun.

One might say that there were three Bertrand Russells. They were: (1) the experimental investigator, (2) the social critic, and (3) the Voltairian satirist. Sometimes Lord Russell kept these three selves in unison. But, more often than not, he allowed the satirist time to tune his strings in a triumphant chord of protest against stupidity no matter in which sphere it appeared.

It was in his role as experimental investigator that he made his monumental contribution to mathematical philosophy which gained for him an international reputation as one of the great mathematicians of the twentieth century. From Socrates to Hume the basic question that has troubled philosophers is, 'Must every event have a cause?' Bertrand Russell was perplexed, and saddened, when he said, 'I hope that some philosopher can suggest a more optimistic conclusion than Hume's view that the 'A' is only associated with 'B'. The social and political problems of World War I, however, turned his attention from philosophy and science to social phenomena, and much of his later writing deals exclusively with social and political problems. He used a swift and sharp wit to express and expose the evil passions in human minds—suspicion, fear, lust for power, hatred, and intolerance—which stand in the way of a more benevolent world. He was an inspired thinker who had just the right measure of wit to spice his wisdom. Lord Russell, however, possessed one cardinal virtue which was rare among social critics: his criticism was always constructive despite, what appeared to some, a destructive tone. He did not wantonly destroy an edifice, nor did he dismantle an institution without showing how to build a Better One. Above all the reader will find Lord Russell scientific, yet humane, hopeful, and thoroughly honest. Lord Russell was, in short, the greatest combiner of *common sense* and *uncommon sense,* the undisputed heir of a tradition in British philosophy that extends from Francis Bacon. Among the many honours that Lord Russell received in addition to the Nobel Prize are the much esteemed Order of Merit, bestowed upon him by King George VI in 1949, and the Sonning Prize for his contribution to European culture by the University of Copenhagen in 1960.

This book is an anthology of witticisms on a variety of topics: psychology, politics, education, religion, ethics, and sex. The selections are taken from a large number of Lord Russell's books and articles. The choice of selections is the editor's, and he is responsible for the abridgement of exposition and argument. No attempt was made to include every witticism available; in his opinion, this is *Bertrand Russell's Best*.

Shortly after this book was first published in 1958, the editor soon discovered that most people, including some eminent book reviewers, were under the impression that Lord Russell was not quite serious when he engaged in satire. The editor was often reminded that: 'surely Lord Russell cannot be serious', to which it seemed useless to argue. But this popular belief is wholly false. As he himself reminded us in the preface to this volume—which was selected from his own writings from almost three-quarters of a century: 'I should not wish to be thought in earnest only when I am solemn.' He is anything but solemn in the pages of this book.

He never flinched from any issue that was unpopular. In 1950, he purposely titled one of his books *Unpopular Essays*. Perhaps he will be remembered best as the philosopher who watched, waited, guided, and understood. No one can ask any more of any philosopher. This book represents just one side of a multigifted mind, a man gifted with the ability to make people laugh—at themselves. This book is devoted entirely to the things which made him *Unpopular*.

On February 2, 1970, the intellectual world lost one of its most distinguished members when Lord Russell died peacefully in his ninety-eighth year. It is interesting to note that no Philosopher of major significance ever lived as long as Lord Russell since the record of Western Philosophy began with Thales in 600 B.C. But it was not to the intellectual world alone that he gave his legacy. Perhaps Lord Russell's greatest gift to mankind was his unfaltering courage and the fearless stand he took in his campaign to preserve humanity. In a way he summed up all his beliefs when he said: 'Remember your humanity and forget the rest.'

Note to 1977 Mentor Edition

BERTRAND RUSSELL wrote a special Preface to the new and completely revised 1971 edition just a few weeks before he died in his 98th year. In the Preface he said: 'It is pleasant news that Professor Egner is publishing a revision of the book *Bertrand Russell's Best*;' and, so it is pleasant news for me, that this book has now been reprinted in 1977. It is a unique tribute to Lord Russell that his own books—well over seventy of them spanning over seven decades—have not only sold millions of copies and been translated into every language of civilized societies, but that Lord Russell's works reached and influenced more people than any other philosopher in modern times. The views of most philosophers go *unread* by the general public, but the philosophy of Bertrand Russell was *read* and *quoted* more often since Western civilization began in Greece.

As I was close to completing this book I asked Lord Russell if I should make any reference to this volume being a *definitive* selection of his *Best* Wit, Wisdom, and Satire, and he said: 'I rather shrink from the word *definitive* chiefly on the grounds that I am not yet dead.' He was then 97 years old. Lord Russell's scope of human life and the quest for certainty was astounding. But, for him, the word, *certainty,* was a bad one because, as he said: '*Nothing deserves certainty.*' This book takes sharp fun on those ideas and institutions once thought to be *Certain*. A feeling of certainty was curiously absent in all of Russell's works.

Robert E. Egner
April, 1977

Meaning of Symbols

SINCE Lord Russell's books have been published in various editions the editor decided not to include the specific page numbers for the extracts in this book. However, in each case the reference source will appear at the end of each extract.

BOOKS

ARTICLES

SPEECHES

BERTRAND RUSSELL'S BEST

CHAPTER I

✦✦✦✦✦✦✦✦✦✦✦✦✦✦✦✦✦✦✦✦✦✦✦✦

Psychology

HUMAN nature has changed little since the time of primitive man. Our understanding of the forces which control behaviour, however, has increased immeasurably with the development of scientific methods of enquiry in the field of psychology. Only a century ago psychology was completely unscientific; now psychology is an independent science, the latest discipline to be separated from philosophy. Lord Russell maintained, however, that our knowledge of psychology was not used to its fullest advantage in solving the ancient problem of how men can live together in peace. The *Good* life he summed up in a single phrase: 'the good life is one inspired by love and guided by knowledge.'

Lord Russell said that the fundamental motives that appeal to most men are 'acquisitiveness', 'vanity', 'rivalry', and 'love of power'. In politics, for example, the springs of human action are derived from these four basic drives. He observed a classical axiom of human behaviour when he noted that man cannot forget the rudiments of his barbaric past despite his recent adventure into the space odyssey. Since 1950 the species man has acquired more knowledge than in all his previous history, yet his remote ancestors still remind him of his primitive past. Must his insatiable appetites be the epitaph of his ultimate folly?

Not often in his long and perhaps multifarious career

did Lord Russell choose to remain free from the main streams of both popular and scientific controversy. For example, his harsh disapproval of traditional organized religion is well documented and known to the literate public. What is generally not known, however, is that his seminal contributions to the evolution of Logic and Mathematics with Whitehead in the early years of the twentieth-century upset, and in fact contradicted, the authoritarian views of Aristotle which had been cached in hoary tradition for over 2,000 years. Russell and Whitehead demonstrated that the basic assumptions and premises of logic and mathematics are identical. Lord Russell refused to remain silent on any issue until death stilled his voice.

Few modern thinkers dared to be as candid in the expression of unwelcomed thoughts as Lord Russell. His attitude was uncompromising: he was not afraid to run the risk of questioning 'sacred' matters in spite of the fact that his free views exposed him to repeated attacks by bigots and obscurantists. Those who fear the embarrassment of having their noble façade dismantled quite naturally rebel against anyone who suggests a critical examination of their motives and beliefs. A number of the selections in this chapter are taken from Lord Russell's Nobel Prize Acceptance Speech, delivered at Stockholm in 1950. In this lecture his keen observation and sharp satires are focused on human passions and their effect upon mankind. Such topics as vanity, power, and the love of excitement are stripped of their customary trappings and laid out in the nude to lie in state.

Many of the things that Lord Russell attacked during his long and often stormy life—his specific attacks on religion, politics, and sex—have not been corrected, but his sharper satires have not been dulled either. Probably the best, and certainly the most succinct description of his literary style is that each sentence of his prose was like a polished gem.

Vanity is a motive of immense potency. Anyone who has much to do with children knows how they are constantly performing some antic, and saying, 'Look at

me.' 'Look at me' is one of the fundamental desires of
the human heart. It can take innumerable forms, from
buffoonery to the pursuit of posthumous fame. There
was a Renaissance Italian princeling who was asked by
the priest on his death-bed if he had anything to repent
of. 'Yes,' he said, 'there is one thing. On one occasion I
had a visit from the Emperor and the Pope simultaneously. I took them to the top of my tower to see the
view, and I neglected the opportunity to throw them
both down, which would have given me immortal
fame.' History does not relate whether the priest gave
him absolution. (N.P.A.S.)

I once befriended two little girls from Esthonia, who
had narrowly escaped death from starvation in a famine. They lived in my family, and of course had plenty
to eat. But they spent all their leisure visiting neigh-
bouring farms and stealing potatoes, which they hoard-
ed. Rockefeller, who in his infancy had experienced
great poverty, spent his adult life in a similar manner.
(N.P.A.S.)

Human beings show their superiority to the brutes by
their capacity for boredom, though I have sometimes thought in examining the apes at the zoo, that
they, perhaps, have the rudiments of this tiresome emotion. However that may be, experience shows that escape from boredom is one of the really powerful desires
of almost all human beings. When white men first effect
contact with some unspoilt race of savages, they offer
them all kinds of benefits, from the light of the gospel
to pumpkin pie. These, however, much as we may
regret it, most savages receive with indifference. What
they really value among the gifts that we bring to them
is intoxicating liquor, which enables them for the first
time in their lives to have the illusion, for a few brief
moments, that it is better to be alive than dead.
(N.P.A.S.)

What vanity needs for its satisfaction is glory, and it is
easy to have glory without power. The people who
enjoy the greatest glory in the United States are film

stars, but they can be put in their place by the committee for Un-American Activities, which enjoys no glory whatever. (N.P.A.S.)

The desire for excitement is very deep-seated in human being especially in males. I suppose that in the hunting stage it was more easily gratified than it has been since. The chase was exciting, war was exciting, courtship was exciting. A savage will manage to commit adultery with a woman while her husband is asleep beside her. This situation, I imagine, is not boring. But with the coming of agriculture life began to grow dull, except, of course, for the aristocrats, who remained, and still remain, in the hunting stage. (C.H.)

The completely untravelled person will view all foreigners as the savage regards a member of another herd. But the man who has travelled, or who has studied international politics, will have discovered that, if the herd is to prosper, it must, to some degree, become amalgamated with other herds. If you are English and someone says to you: 'The French are your brothers,' your first instinctive feeling will be: 'Nonsense, they shrug their shoulders, and talk French. And I am even told that they eat frogs.' If he explains to you that one may have to fight the Russians, that, if so, it will be desirable to defend the line of the Rhine, and that, if the line of the Rhine is to be defended, the help of the French is essential, you will begin to see what he means when he says that the French are your brothers. But if some fellow-traveller were to go on to say that the Russians also are your brothers, he would be unable to persuade you, unless he could show that we are in danger from the Martians. We love those who hate our enemies, and if we had no enemies there would be very few people whom we should love. (N.P.A.S.)

Civilized life has grown altogether too tame, and, if it is to be stable, it must provide harmless outlets for the impulses which our remote ancestors satisfied in hunting. In Australia, where people are few and rabbits are many, I watched a whole populace satisfying the primitive impulse in the primitive manner by the skillful slaughter of many thousands of rabbits. But in London or New York, where people are many and rabbits are few, some other means must be found to gratify primitive impulse. I think every big town should contain artificial waterfalls that people could descend in very fragile canoes, and they should contain bathing pools full of mechanical sharks. Any person found advocating a preventive war should be condemned to two hours a day with these ingenious monsters. (N.P.A.S.)

Every isolated passion is, in isolation, insane; sanity may be defined as a synthesis of insanities. Every dominant passion generates a dominant fear, the fear of its non-fulfillment. Every dominant fear generates a nightmare, sometimes in the form of an explicit and conscious fanaticism, sometimes in a paralysing timidity, sometimes in an unconscious or sub-conscious terror which finds expression only in dreams. The man who wishes to preserve sanity in a dangerous world should summon in his own mind a parliament of fears, in which each in turn is voted absurd by all the others. (N.E.P., introduction.)

The frequency with which a man experiences lust depends upon his own physical condition, whereas the occasions which rouse such feelings in him depend upon the social conventions to which he is accustomed. To an early Victorian man a woman's ankles were sufficient stimulus, whereas a modern man remains unmoved by anything up to the thigh. This is merely a question of fashion in clothing. If nakedness were the fashion, it would cease to excite us, and women would be forced, as they are in certain savage tribes, to adopt clothing as a means of making themselves sexually attractive. Exactly similar considerations apply to literature and pictures: what was exciting in the Victorian Age would leave men of a franker epoch quite unmoved. The more prudes restrict the permissible degree of sexual appeal, the less is required to make such an appeal effective. Nine-tenths of the appeal of pornography is due to the indecent feelings concerning sex which moralists inculcate in the young; the other tenth is physiological, and will occur in one way or another whatever the state of the law may be. On these grounds, although I fear that few will agree with me, I am firmly persuaded that there ought to be no law whatsoever on the subject of obscene publications. (M.M.)

Men who allow their love of power to give them a distorted view of the world are to be found in every asylum: one man will think he is the Governor of the Bank of England, another will think he is the King, and yet another will think he is God. Highly similar delusions, if expressed by educated men in obscure language, lead to professorships of philosophy; and if expressed by emotional men in eloquent language, lead to dictatorships. (P. : A.N.S.A.)

Anthropologists have described how Papuan head hunters, deprived by white authority of their habitual sport, lose all zest, and are no longer able to be interested in anything. I do not wish to infer that they should have been allowed to go on hunting heads, but I do mean that it would have been worth while if psychologists had taken some trouble to find some innocent substitute activity. Civilized Man everywhere is, to some degree, in the position of the Papuan victims of virtue. We have all kinds of aggressive impulses, and also creative impulses, which society forbids us to indulge, and the alternatives that it supplies in the shape of football matches and all-in wrestling are hardly adequate. Anyone who hopes that in time it may be possible to abolish war should give serious thought to the problem of satisfying harmlessly the instincts that we inherit from long generations of savages. For my part I find a sufficient outlet in detective stories, where I alternately identify myself with the murderer and the huntsman-detective, but I know there are those to whom this vicarious outlet is too mild, and for them something stronger should be provided. (A.L.)

In Lisbon when heretics were publicly burned, it sometimes happened that one of them, by a particularly edifying recantation, would be granted the boon of being strangled before being put into the flames. This would make the spectators so furious that the authorities had great difficulty in preventing them from lynching the penitent and burning him on their own account. The spectacle of the writhing torments of the victim was, in fact, one of the principal pleasures to which the populace looked forward to enliven a somewhat drab existence. I cannot doubt that this pleasure greatly contributed to the general belief that the burning of heretics was a righteous act. The same sort of thing applies to war. People who are vigorous and brutal often find war enjoyable, provided that it is a victorious war and that there is not too much interference with rape and plunder. This is a great help in persuading people that wars are righteous. (U.E.)

In order to be happy we require all kinds of supports to our self-esteem. We are human beings; therefore human beings are the purpose of creation. We are Americans; therefore America is God's own country. We are white; and therefore God cursed Ham and his descendants who were black. We are Protestant or Catholic, as the case may be; therefore Catholics or Protestants, as the case may be, are an abomination. We are male; and therefore women are unreasonable; or female; and therefore men are brutes. We are Easterners; and therefore the West is wild and woolly; or Westerners, and therefore the East is effete. We work with our brains; and therefore it is the educated classes that are important; or we work with our hands; and therefore manual labour alone gives dignity. Finally, and above all, we each have one merit which is entirely unique: we are Ourself. With these comforting reflections we go out to do battle with the world; without them our courage might fail. Without them, as things are, we should feel inferior because we have not learned the sentiment of equality. If we could feel genuinely that we are the equals of our neighbours, neither their betters nor their inferiors, perhaps life would become less of a battle, and we should need less in the way of intoxicating myth to give us Dutch courage. (U.E.)

There was, until the end of the eighteenth century, a theory that insanity is due to possession by devils. It was inferred that any pain suffered by the patient is also suffered by the devils, so that the best cure is to make the patient suffer so much that the devils will decide to abandon him. The insane, in accordance with this theory, were savagely beaten. This treatment was tried on King George III when he was mad, but without success. It is a curious and painful fact that almost all the completely futile treatments that have been believed in during the long history of medical folly have been such as caused acute suffering to the patient. When anaesthetics were discovered, pious people considered them an attempt to evade the will of God. It was pointed out, however, that when God extracted Adam's rib He put him into a deep sleep. This proved that anaesthetics are all right for *men*; women, however, ought to suffer because of the curse of Eve. In the West votes for women proved this doctrine mistaken, but in Japan, to this day, women in childbirth are not allowed any alleviation through anaesthetics. As the Japanese do not believe in Genesis, this piece of sadism must have some other justification. (U.E.)

By self-interest Man has become gregarious, but in instinct he has remained to a great extent solitary; hence the need of religion and morality to reinforce self-interest. But the habit of foregoing present satisfactions for the sake of future advantages is irksome, and when passions are roused the prudent restraints of social behaviour become difficult to endure. Those who, at such times, throw them off, acquire a new energy and sense of power from the cessation of inner conflict, and, though they may come to disaster in the end, enjoy meanwhile a sense of god-like exaltation which, though known to the great mystics, can never be experienced by a merely pedestrian virtue. The solitary part of their nature reasserts itself, but if the intellect survives the reassertion must clothe itself in myth. The mystic becomes one with God, and in the contemplation of the infinite feels himself absolved from duty to his neighbour. The anarchic rebel does even better: he feels himself not one with God, but God. Truth and duty, which represent our subjection to matter and to our neighbours, exist no longer for the man who has become God; for others, truth is what *he* posits, duty what *he* commands. If we could all live solitary and without labour, we could all enjoy this ecstasy of independence; since we cannot, its delights are only available to madmen and dictators. (H.W.P.)

Happiness is promoted by associations of persons with similar tastes and similar opinions. Social intercourse may be expected to develop more and more along these lines, and it may be hoped that by these means the loneliness that now afflicts so many unconventional people will be gradually diminished almost to vanishing point. This will undoubtedly increase their happiness, but it will of course diminish the sadistic pleasure which the conventional at present derive from having the unconventional at their mercy. I do not think, however, that this is a pleasure which we need be greatly concerned to preserve. (C.H.)

Our mental make-up is suited to a life of very severe physical labour. I used, when I was younger, to take my holidays walking. I would cover twenty-five miles a day, and when the evening came I had no need of anything to keep me from boredom, since the delight of sitting amply sufficed. But modern life cannot be conducted on these physically strenuous principles. A great deal of work is sedentary, and most manual work exercises only a few specialized muscles. When crowds assemble in Trafalgar Square to cheer to the echo an announcement that the government has decided to have them killed, they would not do so if they had all walked twenty-five miles that day. This cure for bellicosity is, however, impracticable, and if the human race is to survive—a thing which is, perhaps, undesirable—other means must be found for securing an innocent outlet for the unused physical energy that produces love of excitement. This is a matter which has been too little considered, both by moralists and by social reformers.

The social reformers are of the opinion that they have
more serious things to consider. The moralists, on the
other hand, are immensely impressed with the seriousness of all the permitted outlets of the love of excitement; the seriousness, however, in their minds, is that of
Sin. Dance halls, cinemas, this age of jazz, are all, if we
may believe our ears, gateways to Hell, and we should be
better employed sitting at home contemplating our sins.
I find myself unable to be in entire agreement with the
grave men who utter these warnings. The devil has
many forms, some designed to deceive the young, some
designed to deceive the old and serious. If it is the devil
that tempts the young to enjoy themselves, is it not,
perhaps, the same personage that persuades the old to
condemn their enjoyment? And is not condemnation
perhaps merely a form of excitement appropriate to old
age? And is it not, perhaps, a drug which—like opium—
has to be taken in continually stronger doses to produce
the desired effect? Is it not to be feared that, beginning
with the wickedness of the cinema, we should be led
step by step to condemn the opposite political party,
dagoes, wops, Asiatics, and, in short, everybody except
the fellow members of our club? And it is from just
such condemnations, when widespread, that wars proceed. I have never heard of a war that proceeded from
dance halls. (N.P.A.S.)

There is no greater reason for children to honour parents than for parents to honour children, except that
while the children are young, the parents are stronger
than the children. The same thing, of course, happened
in the relations of men and women. It was the duty of
wives to submit to husbands, not of husbands to submit
to wives. The only basis for this view was that if wives
could be induced to accept it, it saved trouble for their
husbands. 'The man is not of the woman, but the
woman of the man; neither was the man created for the
woman, but the woman for the man' (I Cor. xi. 8, 9). I
defy anyone to find a basis for this view, except that
men have stronger muscles than women. (N.H.C.W.)

A large proportion of the human race, it is true, is

obliged to work so hard in obtaining necessaries that little energy is left over for other purposes; but those whose livelihood is assured do not, on that account, cease to be active. Xerxes had no lack of food or raiment or wives at the time when he embarked upon the Athenian expedition. Newton was certain of material comfort from the moment when he became a Fellow of Trinity, but it was after this that he wrote the *Principia*. St Francis and Ignatius Loyola had no need to found Orders to escape from want. These were eminent men, but the same characteristic, in varying degrees, is to be found in all but a small exceptionally sluggish minority. Mrs A, who is quite sure of her husband's success in business, and has no fear of the workhouse, likes to be better dressed than Mrs B, although she could escape the danger of pneumonia at much less expense. (P.:A.N.S.A.)

Some astronomers try to cheer us up in moments of depression by assuring us that one fine day the sun will explode, and in the twinkling of an eye we shall all be turned into gas. I do not know whether this is going to happen, nor when it will happen if it does happen, but I think it is safe to say that if it does it will be a matter outside human control, and that even the best astronomers will be unable to prevent it. This is an extreme example, and one which it is useless to think about, because there is no way in which human behaviour can be adapted to it. It does, however, serve one purpose, which is to remind us that we are not gods. You may exclaim indignantly, 'but I never thought we were!' No doubt, dear reader, you are not one of those who suffer from the most extreme follies of our age, for if you were, you would not be one of my readers. But if you consider the Politbureau or the American technocrats you will see that there are those who escape atheism by impiously imagining themselves on the throne of the Almighty. (N.H.C.W.)

Mass hysteria is a phenomenon not confined to human beings; it may be seen in any gregarious species. I once saw a photograph of a large herd of wild elephants in

Central Africa seeing an aeroplane for the first time, and all in a state of wild collective terror. The elephant, at most times, is a calm and sagacious beast, but this unprecedented phenomenon of a noisy, unknown animal in the sky had thrown the whole herd completely off its balance. Each separate animal was terrified, and its terror communicated itself to the others, causing a vast multiplication of panic. As, however, there were no journalists among them, the terror died down when the aeroplane was out of sight. (T.H.D.H.)

The criminal law has, from the point of view of thwarted virtue, the merit of allowing an outlet for those impulses of aggression which cowardice, disguised as morality, restrains in their more spontaneous forms. War has the same merit. You must not kill your neighbour, whom perhaps you genuinely hate, but by a little propaganda this hate can be transferred to some foreign nation, against whom all your murderous impulses become patriotic herosim. (N.H.C.W.)

If you ask a modern anti-Semite why he dislikes Jews, he will tell you that they are unscrupulous and sharp in business and merciless to their debtors; he will tell you that they are always on the make, always intriguing, always supporting each other against Gentile competitors. If you say you have sometimes found similar characteristics among Christians, the anti-Semite will say: 'Oh, of course I don't deny there are ruffians who are not Jews. And I have some very good friends among Jews. But I am speaking of the average.' If you question him when he is off his guard, you will find that whenever a Jew engages in a bit of sharp practice he says, 'how like a Jew,' but when a Gentile does likewise he says 'and, you know, the astonishing thing is that he is not a Jew.' This is not a scientific method of arriving at averages. (N.H.C.W.)

Young men and young women meet each other with much less difficulty than was formerly the case, and every house-maid expects at least once a week as much excitement as would have lasted a Jane Austen heroine throughout a whole novel. (c.h.)

Everybody has had at some time nightmares of falling, which seem to suggest an origin in the lives of our arboreal ancestors, though this perhaps is fanciful. Hymns and myths tend to speak of refuges from storm and of images of water in a parched land. Moses striking the rock makes a universal appeal, even to those who have never been very thirsty. Hymns represent heaven as a refuge from the storms of life, not as a place where one escapes the dangers of being run over by a motor-bus, although the latter danger is a much more frequent experience in modern urban life. (n.h.c.w.)

Now, apart from arguments as to the proved fallibility of memory, there is one awkward consideration which the sceptic may urge. Remembering, which occurs now, cannot possibly—he may say—prove that what is remembered occurred at some other time, because the world might have sprung into being five minutes ago, exactly as it then was, full of acts of remembering which were entirely misleading. Opponents of Darwin, such as Edmund Grosse's father, urged a very similar argument against evolution. The world, they said, was created in 4004 b.c., complete with fossils, which were inserted to try our faith. The world was created suddenly, but was made such as it would have been if it had evolved. There is no logical impossibility about this view. And similarly there is no logical impossibility in the view that the world was created five minutes ago, complete with memories and records. This may seem an improbable hypothesis, but it is not logically refutable. (o.p.)

If I wish to travel by plane to New York, reason tells me that it is better to take a plane which is going to New York than one which is going to Constantinople. I suppose that those who think me unduly rational, consider that I ought to become so agitated at the airport as to jump into the first plane that I see, and when it lands me in Constantinople I ought to curse the people among whom I find myself for being Turks and not Americans. This would be a fine, full-blooded way of behaving, and would, I suppose, meet with the commendation of my critics. (H.S.E.P.)

My first advice on how *not* to grow old would be to choose your ancestors carefully. Although both my parents died young, I have done well in this respect as regards my other ancestors. My maternal grandfather, it is true, was cut off in the flower of his youth at the age of sixty-seven, but my other three grandparents all lived to be over eighty. Of remoter ancestors I can only discover one who did not live to a great age, and he died of a disease which is now rare, namely, having his head cut off. (P.F.M.)

The difference between mind and brain is not a difference of quality, but a difference of arrangement. It is like the difference between arranging people in geographical order or in alphabetical order, both of which are done in the post office directory. The same people are arranged in both cases, but in quite different contexts. In like manner the context of a visual sensation for physics is physical, and outside the brain. Going backward, it takes you to the eye, and thence to a photon and thence to a quantum transition in some distant object. The context of the visual sensation for psychology is quite different. Suppose, for example, the visual sensation is that of a telegram saying that you are ruined. A number of events will take place in your mind in accordance with the laws of psychological causation, and it may be quite a long time before there is any purely physical effect, such as tearing your hair, or exclaiming 'Woe is me!' (P.F.M.)

The unemployed rich are an evil of a special sort. The world is full of idle people, mostly women, who have little education, much money, and consequently great self-confidence. Owing to their wealth, they are able to cause much labour to be devoted to their comfort. Although they seldom have any genuine culture, they are the chief patrons of art, which is not likely to please them unless it is bad. (I.P.I.)

Boredom is not to be regarded as wholly evil. There are two sorts, of which one is fructifying, while the other is stultifying. The fructifying kind arises from the absence of drugs, and the stultifying kind from the absence of vital activities. (C.H.)

Every man would like to be God, if it were possible; some few find it difficult to admit the impossibility. (P.:A.N.S.A.)

The newspapers, at one time, said that I was dead, but after carefully examining the evidence I came to the conclusion that the statement was false. When the statement comes first and the evidence afterwards, there is a process called 'verification' which involves confrontation of the statement with the evidence. (I.M.T.)

CHAPTER II

◆◆◆◆◆◆◆◆◆◆◆◆◆◆◆◆◆◆◆◆◆

Religion

WITH the publication in 1903 of Lord Russell's now celebrated essay, 'A Free Man's Worship', his views on religion were followed avidly by most writers on this subject. In fact this one essay became a classic and one of the most quoted in twentieth-century literature. His views on religion remained the same since he was fifteen years old but the evidence for belief in traditional religious dogma has never undergone any great changes either, in spite of apologetics for ecumenical reform. Lord Russell was a patient man. He never opposed those 'for whom mythology is a cultural characteristic; he did, however, repeatedly attack those who adopted various psychological and physical means of persecuting their opponents in propagating their myths.

Lord Russell regarded religion as a disease. He was a tiny bit curious about the effects of religious training on the young and suggested a prescription for the disease which wise Patriarchs should remember: 'Catch them,' he said, 'while they are young.' However, if one cannot catch them while they are young, a wise benevolent father can take out fire insurance on their Souls. Lord Russell was convinced that many people enjoy the comforts of religious myths because many people enjoy an extended vacation from evidence. As Professor Obelsky observed, if scarcity were absent, there would be no need for economic theory. Lord Russell observed that religion would die out if people solved their social problems.

The history of organized religion in the West affords a number of instances in which religion has opposed humanitarian and scientific progress. A number of advances in medicine, for example, would have been achieved sooner if free inquiry had been common and orthodox thinking habits had been rare. Only a century ago there were many who believed that certain diseases were caused by sin, and that it was good that the wicked ought to suffer for their sins. Anyone who dared suggest some other cause of these diseases was subject to various forms of censorship. People in Western countries are not burned at the stake for disagreeing with prevailing religious dogma as they were in former times, but they are still subject to other, more refined, forms of unkindness. The psychological impact on religious minorities, especially on the younger members of these groups, of being merely 'tolerated' by the majority group is a case in point. Agnostics, for instance, are not always entirely free to admit their beliefs publicly without suffering some kind of unpleasant consequences. In some cases this may mean discrimination in obtaining employment by one who is otherwise fully qualified, while in other cases it may mean a little loss in standing, or kneeling, in a community if it were known that one confessed the final sin—not believing in God. Those who claim with triumphant rhetoric that religious freedom is a necessary condition for a democratic culture, however large or small, sometimes forget that tolerance means more than a concordat between the adherents of rival creeds. Religious liberty, we are told, is something to cherish, but this ideal ought to be extended to those who profess no dogma whatever.

It should be observed that Ecumenical Councils have been somewhat disappointing in bringing Christians together in loving embrace. Even in the Roman Catholic church, which has celebrated a long history of persecution of other Christians, right and left wing groups now battle to find out if celibacy is as virtuous as was once supposed. Bertrand Russell found himself unable to be in entire agreement with some points of Catholic beliefs. The Church *Herself* is caught in a unique sexual posture. For example, shall laymen be permitted to continue intercourse for purely procreative purposes in front of a poverty-stricken audience, or, perhaps, shall nuns and priests be permitted to let the whole idea die from '*Natural Law*'? Very exciting, indeed! However, these pleasant thoughts ought not to remind one of sin in India, China, and South America. But, we must not be too critical of the official Expert on Sin since St Thomas could not have forecast the population dilemma he created in his own club. Shortly before his death in 1274, his *Eminence*, St Thomas, warned all the fellow members of his club that henceforth sexual pleasures must be considered wicked. One might suppose that the Saint did not often enjoy a few brief moments of *Natural* pleasure.

Since the beginning of human events religion has in various manifestations dominated man's conscious effort to make some kind of sense out of his sudden adventure into what he has always considered the 'unknown'. Lord Russell never faltered, however, from his belief that religion has done more harm than good as the pages of repeated history reveal. He thought that the apologists for religion are caught in an unusual dilemma. For instance, the thought of *death,* at first, seems rather awesome, but religion offers great comforts for the living; to the dead, however, religion does not seem to have much significance. The arguments in support of the dead have not been heard. *Heaven* seems to be a delightful place but one must imagine that it would be somewhat boring on a permanent basis. *Hell* is not a bright prospect either, but suppose that *Purgatory* were possible: one could have a chance to visit both Heaven and Hell, and then exchange pleasantries. There is also the possibility that one could leave the children in Limbo, without pain of mortal sin. In his book *Why I Am Not a Christian*, he reaffirmed his basic conviction that 'all religions are both harmful and untrue'. Religion, if it is not to be harmful, must be free of dangerous elements—suspicion, fear, and hate—which lead step by step to escalate organized persecution.

The selections which follow illustrate that he wasted

no time in performing open surgery on man's religious myths. He found some absurdities which now seem almost incredible. In sharp satires let us look at some puzzling illustrations—some are still puzzling.

I observe that a very large portion of the human race does not believe in God and suffers no visible punishment in consequence. And if there were a God, I think it very unlikely that he would have such an uneasy vanity as to be offended by those who doubt his existence. (W.A.)

Although we are taught the Copernican astronomy in our textbooks, it has not yet penetrated to our religion or our morals, and has not even succeeded in destroying belief in astrology. People still think that the Divine Plan has special reference to human beings, and that a Special Providence not only looks after the good, but also punishes the wicked. I am sometimes shocked by the blasphemies of those who think themselves pious— for instance, the nuns who never take a bath without wearing a bathrobe all the time. When asked why, since no man can see them, they reply: 'Oh, but you forget the good God.' Apparently they conceive of the Deity as a Peeping Tom, whose omnipotence enables Him to see through bathroom walls, but who is foiled by bathrobes. This view strikes me as curious. (U.E.)

Christians hold that their faith does good, but other faiths do harm. At any rate, they hold this about the Communist faith. What I wish to maintain is that *all* faiths do harm. We may define 'faith' as a firm belief in something for which there is no evidence. When there is evidence, no one speaks of 'faith'. We do not speak of faith that two and two are four or that the earth is round. We only speak of faith when we wish to substitute emotion for evidence. (H.S.E.P.)

The Church attacked the habit of the bath on the ground that everything which makes the body more attractive tends towards sin. Dirt was praised, and the odour of sanctity became more and more penetrating. 'The purity of the body and its garments,' said St Paula, 'means the impurity of the soul.' (Havelock Ellis, *Studies in the Psychology of Sex*, Vol. IV, p. 31.) Lice were called the pearls of God, and to be covered with them was an indispensable mark of a holy man. (M.M.)

Since evolution became fashionable, the glorification of Man has taken a new form. We are told that evolution has been guided by one great Purpose: through the millions of years when there were only slime, or trilobites, throughout the ages of dinosaurs and giant ferns, of bees and wild flowers, God was preparing the Great Climax. At last, in the fulness of time, He produced Man, including such specimens as Nero and Caligula, Hitler and Mussolini, whose transcendent glory justified the long painful process. For my part, I find even eternal damnation less incredible, certainly less ridiculous, than this lame and impotent conclusion which we are asked to admire as the supreme effort of Omnipotence. (U.E.)

It is not by prayer and humility that you cause things to go as you wish, but by acquiring a knowledge of natural laws. The power you acquire in this way is much greater and more reliable than that formerly supposed to be acquired by prayer, because you never could tell whether your prayer would be favourably heard in Heaven. The power of prayer, moreover, had recognized limits; it would have been impious to ask too much. But the power of science has no known limits. We were told that faith could remove mountains, but no one believed it; we are now told that the atomic bomb can remove mountains, and everyone believes it. (I.S.S.)

According to St Thomas the soul is not transmitted with the semen, but is created afresh with each man. There is, it is true, a difficulty: when a man is born out of wedlock, this seems to make God an accomplice in adultery. This objection, however, is only specious. There is a grave objection which troubled St Augustine, and that is as to the transmission of original sin. It is the soul that sins, and if the soul is not transmitted, but created afresh, how can it inherit the sin of Adam? This is not discussed by St Thomas. (H.W.P.)

I am constantly asked: What can you, with your cold rationalism, offer to the seeker after salvation that is comparable to the cosy homelike comfort of a fenced-in dogmatic creed? To this the answer is many-sided. In the first place, I do not say that I can offer as much happiness as is to be obtained by the abdication of reason. I do not say that I can offer as much happiness as is to be obtained from drink or drugs or amassing great wealth by swindling widows and orphans. It is not the happiness of the individual convert that concerns me; it is the happiness of mankind. If you genuinely desire the happiness of mankind, certain forms of ignoble personal happiness are not open to you. If your child is ill, and you are a conscientious parent, you accept medical diagnosis, however doubtful and discouraging; if you accept the cheerful opinion of a quack and your child consequently dies, you are not excused by the pleasantness of belief in the quack while it lasted. (I.S.S.)

If everything must have a cause, then God must have a cause. If there can be anything without a cause, it may just as well be the world as God, so that there cannot be any validity in that argument. It is exactly of the same nature as the Indian's view, that the world rested upon an elephant and the elephant rested upon a tortoise; and when they said, 'How about the tortoise?' the Indian said, 'Suppose we change the subject.' The argument is really no better than that. (W.N.C.)

The agnostic is not quite so certain as some Christians are as to what is good and what is evil. He does not hold, as most Christians in the past held, that people who disagree with the Government on abstruse points of theology ought to suffer a painful death. He is against persecution, and rather chary of moral condemnation.

As for 'sin', he thinks it not a useful notion. He admits, of course, that some kinds of conduct are desirable and some undesirable, but he holds that the punishment of undesirable kinds is only to be commended when it is deterrent or reformatory, not when it is inflicted because it is thought a good thing on its own account that the wicked should suffer. It was this belief in vindictive punishment that made men accept hell. This is part of the harm done by the notion of 'sin'. (W.A.)

It was geology, Darwin, and the doctrine of evolution, that first upset the faith of British men of science. If man was evolved by insensible gradations from lower forms of life, a number of things became very difficult to understand. At what moment in evolution did our ancestors acquire free will? At what stage in the long journey from the amoeba did they begin to have immortal souls? When did they first become capable of the kinds of wickedness that would justify a benevolent Creator in sending them into eternal torment? Most people felt that such punishment would be hard on monkeys, in spite of their propensity for throwing coconuts at the heads of Europeans. But how about *Pithecanthropus Erectus?* Was it really he who ate the apple? Or was it *Homo Pekiniensis?* Or was it perhaps the Piltdown man? I went to Piltdown once, but saw no evidence of special depravity in that village, nor did I see any signs of its having changed appreciably since prehistoric ages. Perhaps then it was the Neanderthal men who first sinned? This seems the more likely, as they lived in Germany. But obviously there can be no answer to such questions, and those theologians who do not wholly reject evolution have had to make profound readjustments. (U.E.)

There is something feeble and a little contemptible about a man who cannot face the perils of life without the help of comfortable myths. Almost inevitably some part of him is aware that they are myths and that he believes them only because they are comforting. But he dare not face this thought! Moreover, since he is aware, however dimly, that his opinions are not rational, he becomes furious when they are disputed. (H.S.E.P.)

What Galileo and Newton had done for astronomy Darwin did for biology. The adaptations of animals and plants to their environments were a favourite theme of pious naturalists in the eighteenth and early nineteenth centuries. These adaptations were explained by the Divine Purpose. It is true that the explanation was sometimes a little odd. If rabbits were theologians, they might think the exquisite adaptation of weasels to the killing of rabbits hardly a matter for thankfulness. And there was a conspiracy of silence about the tapeworm. (I.S.S.)

I do not understand where the 'beauty' and 'harmony' of nature are supposed to be found. Throughout the animal kingdom, animals ruthlessly prey upon each other. Most of them are either cruelly killed by other animals or slowly die of hunger. For my part, I am unable to see any very great beauty or harmony in the tapeworm. Let it not be said that this creature is sent as a punishment for our sins, for it is more prevalent among animals than among humans.

I suppose what is meant by this 'beauty' and 'harmony' are such things as the beauty of the starry heavens. But one should remember that the stars every now and again explode and reduce everything in their neighbourhood to a vague mist. (W.A.)

One of the last questions discussed by St Thomas in book four is the resurrection of the body. Here, as elsewhere, Aquinas states very fairly the arguments that have been brought against orthodox position. One of these, at first sight, offers great difficulties. What is to happen, asks the Saint, to a man who never, throughout his life, ate anything but human flesh, and whose parents did likewise? It would seem unfair to his victims that they should be deprived of their bodies at the last day as a consequence of his greed; yet, if not, what will be left to make up his body? I am happy to say that this difficulty, which might at first sight seem insuperable, is triumphantly met. The identity of the body, Saint Thomas points out, is not dependent on the persistence of the same material particles; during life, by the processes of eating and digesting, the matter composing the body undergoes perpetual change. The cannibal may, therefore, receive the same body at the resurrection, even if it is not composed of the same matter as was in his body when he died. With this comforting thought we may end our abstract of the *Summa contra Gentiles*. (H.W.P.)

There is little of the true philosophic spirit in Aquinas. He does not, like the Platonic Socrates, set out to follow wherever the argument may lead. He is not engaged in an inquiry, the result of which it is impossible to know in advance. Before he begins to philosophize, he already knows the truth; it is declared in the Catholic faith. If he can find apparently rational arguments for some part of the faith, so much the better; if he cannot, he need only fall back on revelation. The finding of arguments for a conclusion given in advance is not philosophy, but special pleading. (H.W.P.)

The raw fruits of the earth were made for human sustenance. Even the white tails of rabbits, according to some theologians, have a purpose, namely to make it easier for sportsmen to shoot them. There are, it is true, some inconveniences: lions and tigers are too fierce, the summer is too hot, and the winter too cold. But these things only began after Adam ate the apple; before that, all animals were vegetarians, and the season was always spring. If only Adam had been content with peaches and nectarines, grapes and pears and pineapples, these blessings would still be ours. (U.E.)

According to Saint Thomas, astrology is to be rejected, for the usual reasons. In answer to the question 'Is there such a thing as fate?' Aquinas replies that we *might* give the name 'fate' to the order impressed by Providence, but it is wiser not to do so, as 'fate' is a pagan word. This leads to an argument that prayer is useful although Providence is unchangeable (I have failed to follow this argument), God sometimes works miracles, but no one else can. Magic, however, is possible with the help of demons; this is not properly miraculous, and is not by the help of the stars. (H.W.P.)

How far has the American outlook on life and the world influenced Europe, and how far is it likely to do so?

And first of all: What is the distinctively European outlook?

Traditionally, the European outlook may be said to be derived from astronomy. When Abraham watched his flocks by night, he observed the stars in their courses: they moved with a majestic regularity utterly remote from human control. When the Lord answered Job out of the whirlwind, He said: 'Canst thou bind the sweet influences of Pleiades, or loose the bands of Orion?' The reply was in the negative. Even more relevant is the question: 'Knowest thou the ordinances of heaven? Canst thou set the dominion thereof in the earth?' To which Job answered: 'Behold, I am vile; what shall I answer thee? I will lay my hand upon my mouth.' The conclusion is that man is a feeble creature, to whom only submission and worship are becoming. Pride is insolence, and belief in human power is impiety. (P.C.I.)

Nature, it is true, still sees to it that we are mortal, but with the progress in medicine it will become more and more common for people to live until they have had their fill of life. We are supposed to wish to live forever and to look forward to the unending joys of heaven, of which, by miracle, the monotony will never grow stale. But, in fact, if you question any candid person who is no longer young, he is very likely to tell you that, having tasted life in this world, he has no wish to begin again as a 'new boy' in another. (U.E.)

We read in the Old Testament that it was a religious duty to exterminate conquered races completely, and that to spare even their cattle and sheep was an impiety. Dark terrors and misfortunes in the life to come oppressed the Egyptians and Etruscans, but never reached their full development until the victory of Christianity. Gloomy saints who abstained from all pleasures of sense, who lived in solitude in the desert, denying themselves meat and wine and the society of women, were, nevertheless, not obliged to abstain from *all* pleasures. The pleasures of the mind were considered to be superior to those of the body, and a high place among the pleasures of the mind was assigned to the contemplation of the eternal tortures to which the pagans and heretics would hereafter be subjected. (U.E.)

The standpoint of modern liberal theologians is well set forth by Dr Tennant in his book *The Concept of Sin.* According to him sin consists in acts of will that are in conscious opposition to a known law, the moral law being known by Revelation as God's will. It follows that a man destitute of religion cannot sin. (H.S.E.P.)

One occasion for theological intervention to prevent the mitigation of human suffering was the discovery of anaesthetics. Simpson, in 1847, recommended their use in childbirth, and was immediately reminded by the clergy that God said to Eve: 'In sorrow shalt thou bring forth children' (Gen. iii. 16). And how could she sorrow if she was under the influence of chloroform? Simpson succeeded in proving that there was no harm in giving anaesthetics to *men*, because God put Adam into a deep sleep when He extracted his rib. But male ecclesiastics remained unconvinced as regards the sufferings of *women*, at any rate in childbirth. (R.S.)

The conception of purpose is a natural one to apply to a human artificer. A man who desires a house cannot, except in the Arabian Nights, have it rise before him as a result of his mere wish; time and labour must be expended before his wish can be gratified. But Omnipotence is subject to no such limitations. If God really thinks well of the human race—an unplausible hypothesis, as it seems to me—why not proceed, as in Genesis, to create man at once? What was the point of the ichthyosaurs, dinosaurs, diplodochi, mastodons, and so on? Dr Barnes himself confesses, somewhere, that the purpose of the tapeworm is a mystery. What useful purpose is served by rabies and hydrophobia? It is no answer to say that the laws of nature inevitably produce evil as well as good, for God decreed the laws of nature. The evil which is due to sin may be explained as the result of our free will, but the problem of evil in the pre-human world remains. I hardly think Dr Barnes will accept the solution offered by William Gillespie, that the bodies of beasts of prey were inhabited by devils, whose first sins antedated the brute creation; yet it is difficult to see what other logically satisfying answer can be suggested. The difficulty is old, but none the less real. An omnipotent Being who created a world containing evil not due to sin must Himself be at least partially evil. (R.S.)

The Greek Church is blamed for denying the double procession of the Holy Ghost and the supremacy of the Pope. We are warned that, although Christ was conceived of the Holy Ghost, we must not suppose that He was the son of the Holy Ghost according to the flesh. (H.W.P.)

Belief in God and a future life makes it possible to go through life with less of stoic courage than is needed by sceptics. A great many young people lose faith in these dogmas at an age at which despair is easy, and thus have to face a much more intense unhappiness than that which falls to the lot of those who have never had a religious upbringing. Christianity offers reasons for not fearing death or the universe, and in so doing it fails to teach adequately the virtue of courage. The craving for religious faith being largely an outcome of fear, the advocates of faith tend to think that certain kinds of fear are not to be deprecated. In this, to my mind, they are gravely mistaken. To allow oneself to entertain pleasant beliefs as a means of avoiding fear is not to live in the best way. In so far as religion makes its appeal to fear, it is lowering to human dignity. (E.S.O.)

The whole conception of God is a conception derived from the ancient Oriental despotisms. It is a conception quite unworthy of free men. When you hear people in church debasing themselves and saying that they are miserable sinners, and all the rest of it, it seems contemptible and not worthy of self-respecting human beings. We ought to stand up and look the world frankly in the face. We ought to make the best we can of the world, and if it is not so good as we wish, after all it will still be better than what these others have made of it in all these ages. A good world needs knowledge, kindliness, and courage; it does not need a regretful hankering after the past, or a fettering of the free intelligence by the words uttered long ago by ignorant men. (W.N.C.)

Religion is based, I think, primarily and mainly upon fear. It is partly the terror of the unknown, and partly the wish to feel that you have a kind of elder brother who will stand by you in all your troubles and disputes. Fear is the basis of the whole thing—fear of the mysterious, fear of defeat, fear of death. Science can help us to get over this craven fear in which mankind has lived for so many generations. Science can teach us, and I think our own hearts can teach us, no longer to look round for imaginary supports, no longer to invent allies in the sky, but rather to look to our own efforts here below to make this world a fit place to live in, instead of the sort of place that the Churches in all these centuries have made it. (W.N.C.)

Owing to their miraculous powers, priests (in the eleventh century) could determine whether a man should spend eternity in heaven or in hell. If he died while excommunicate, he went to hell; if he died after priests had performed all the proper ceremonies, he would ultimately go to heaven provided he had duly repented and confessed. Before going to heaven, however, he would have to spend some time—perhaps a very long time—suffering the pains of purgatory. Priests could shorten this time by saying masses for his soul, which

they were willing to do for a suitable money payment.
(H.W.P.)

Sir James Jeans considers it very doubtful whether, at
the present time, there is life anywhere else. Before the
Copernican revolution, it was natural to suppose that
God's purposes were specially concerned with the earth,
but now this has become an unplausible hypothesis.
If it is the purpose of the Cosmos to evolve mind,
we must regard it as rather incompetent in having
produced so little in such a long time. If we accept the
rather curious view that the Cosmic Purpose is specially
concerned with our little planet, we still find that there
is reason to doubt whether it intends quite what the
theologians say it does. The earth (unless we use
enough poison gas to destroy all life) is likely to remain
habitable for some considerable time, but not for ever.
Perhaps our atmosphere will gradually fly off into
space; perhaps the tides will cause the earth to turn
always the same face to the sun, so that one hemisphere
will be too hot and the other too cold; perhaps (as in a
moral tale by J. B. S. Haldane) the moon will tumble
into the earth. If none of these things happens first, we
shall in any case be all destroyed when the sun ex-
plodes and becomes a cold white dwarf, which, we are
told by Jeans, is to happen in about a million million
years, though the exact date is still somewhat uncertain.

A million million years gives us some time to prepare
for the end, and we may hope that in the meantime
both astronomy and gunnery will have made considerable progress. The astronomers may have discovered
another star with habitable planets, and the gunners
may be able to fire us off to it with a speed approaching
that of light, in which case, if the passengers were all
young to begin with, some might arrive before dying of
old age. It is perhaps a slender hope, but let us make
the best of it. (R.S.)

I do not believe that a decay of dogmatic belief can do
anything but good. I admit at once that new systems of
dogma, such as those of the Nazis and the Communists, are even worse than the old systems, but they

could never have acquired a hold over men's minds if orthodox dogmatic habits had not been instilled in youth. Stalin's language is full of reminiscences of the theological seminary in which he received his training. What the world needs is not dogma, but an attitude of scientific inquiry, combined with a belief that the torture of millions is not desirable, whether inflicted by Stalin or by a Deity imagined in the likeness of the believer. (H.S.E.P.)

For four and a half months in 1918 I was in prison for pacifist propaganda; but, by the intervention of Arthur Balfour, I was placed in the first division, so that while in prison I was able to read and write as much as I liked, provided I did no pacifist propaganda. I found prison in many ways quite agreeable. I had no engagements, no difficult decisions to make, no fear of callers, no interruptions to my work. I read enormously; I wrote a book, *Introduction to Mathematical Philosophy*, and began the work for *Analysis of Mind*. I was rather interested in my fellow prisoners, who seemed to me in no way morally inferior to the rest of the population, though they were on the whole slightly below the usual level of intelligence, as was shown by their having been caught. For anybody not in the first division, especially for a person accustomed to reading and writing, prison is a severe and terrible punishment; but for me, thanks to Arthur Balfour, this was not so. I was much cheered on my arrival by the warder at the gate, who had to take particulars about me. He asked my religion, and I replied 'agnostic'. He asked how to spell it, and remarked with a sigh: 'Well, there are many religions, but I suppose they all worship the same God'. This remark kept me cheerful for about a week. (P.F.M.)

The most influential school of philosophy in Britain at the present day maintains a certain linguistic doctrine to which I am unable to subscribe. I do not wish to misrepresent this school, but I suppose any opponent of any doctrine is thought to misrepresent it by those who hold it. The doctrine, as I understand it, consists in maintaining that the language of daily life, with words used in their ordinary meanings, suffices for philosophy, which has no need of technical terms or of changes in the signification of common terms. I find myself totally unable to accept this view.

Orthodox Christianity asserts that we survive death. What does it mean by this assertion? And in what sense, if any, is the assertion true? The philosophers with whom I am concerned will consider the first of these questions, but will say that the second is none of their business. I agree entirely that, in this case, a discussion as to what is meant is important and highly necessary as a preliminary to a consideration of the substantial question, but if nothing can be said on the substantial question, it seems a waste of time to discuss what it means. These philosophers remind me of the shop-keeper of whom I once asked the shortest way to Winchester. He called to a man in the back premises:

'Gentleman wants to know the shortest way to Winchester.'

'Winchester?' an unseen voice replied.

'Aye.'

'Way to Winchester?'

'Aye.'

'Shortest way?'

'Aye.'

'Dunno.'

He wanted to get the nature of the question clear, but took no interest in answering it. This is exactly what modern philosophy does for the earnest seeker after truth. Is it surprising that young people turn to other studies? (P.F.M.)

I say people who feel they must have a faith or religion in order to face life are showing a kind of cowardice, which in any other sphere would be considered contemptible. But when it is in the religious sphere it is thought admirable, and I cannot admire cowardice whatever sphere it is in. (B.R.S.M.)

There has been a rumour in recent years to the effect that I have become less opposed to religious orthodoxy than I formerly was. This rumour is totally without foundation. I think all the great religions of the world—Buddhism, Hinduism, Christianity, Islam and Communism—both untrue and harmful. It is evident as a matter of logic that, since they disagree, not more than one of them can be true. With very few exceptions, the religion which a man accepts is that of the community in which he lives, which makes it obvious that the influence of environment is what has led him to accept the religion in question. (w.n.c. Preface.)

There is one very serious defect to my mind in Christ's moral character, and that is that He believed in Hell. I do not myself feel that any person who is really profoundly humane can believe in everlasting punishment. Christ certainly as depicted in the Gospels did believe in everlasting punishment, and one does find repeatedly a vindictive fury against those people who would not listen to His preaching—an attitude which is not uncommon with preachers. (w.n.c.)

The view that modern Christians for the most part do not believe in the Bible does not seem to me quite valid. For example, the Anglican Communion still demands a fundamentalist attitude to the Bible. Many Christians do not seem to know that in the service for the Ordering of Deacons the Bishop says: 'Do you unfeignedly believe all the Canonical Scriptures of the Old and New Testament?' And the Ordinand has to answer: 'I do believe them.' You may say, no doubt, that this does not matter, since no one expects a parson to speak the truth about important matters on solemn occasions. But, for my part, I think it a pity that people who are intended to stand for virtue have to begin their career by a solemn lie. (D.B.R.)

I should like to make clear that I am not a Christian, and have not been a Christian since the age of fifteen. Throughout my life I have made every effort to let it be known that I am not a Christian, and why I am not a Christian. I hope that this will settle all argument: it is not a question about which there has ever been ground for dispute. (D.B.R.)

I think that in philosophical strictness at the level where one doubts the existence of material objects and holds that the world may have existed for only five minutes, I ought to call myself an agnostic; but, for all practical purposes, I am an atheist. I do not think the existence of the Christian God any more probable than the existence of the Gods of Olympus or Valhalla. To take another illustration: nobody can prove that there is not between Earth and Mars a china teapot revolving in an elliptic orbit, but nobody thinks this sufficiently likely to be taken into account in practice. I think the Christian God just as unlikely. (D.B.R.)

In the year 1921 I had double pneumonia in Peking and only one English nurse was obtainable. She was a lady of great piety who told me while I was convalescent that she had had great struggles with her conscience on the ground that she thought it her duty to let me die although professional instinct proved too strong for this virtuous impulse. I was delirious for a fortnight and as soon as the delirium ended I had no recollection whatever of the two weeks that had passed. During these two weeks the aforesaid nurse looked after me at night and my wife looked after me by day. It appears that when I coughed I was in the habit of lapsing into profanity in ways which the nurse mistook for serious appeals to the Deity. (A.B.R.)

You will I think be compelled to admit that in the West influential persons calling themselves Christians have almost a monopoly of tolerance. I consider the official Catholic attitude on divorce, birth control, and censorship exceedingly dangerous to mankind. General Franco, whom Sir Winston Churchill praised as a 'gallant Christian gentleman', has forbidden any work of fiction alluding to adultery, though I believe he had made a special exception for the *Iliad*. (D.B.R.)

People are apt to speak as if the Church throughout history had been kindly, and had shown some respect for the outlook of its Founder, but if you will ask yourself by what process the cruelties of the Middle Ages have been mitigated—for example the burning of heretics and witches—you will find that the protagonists in every campaign for mercy have been unorthodox. The Church, as long as it dared, impeded the progress of medicine by frowning on dissection. The Church was so shocked by geology that the Sorbonne condemned Buffon for maintaining that some present-day mountains are not as old as the world. The Church in recent years has been softening its doctrines on eternal damnation, but it has done so entirely owing to attacks from the unorthodox. In the present day, the opposition of the Church to birth control, if it could be successful, would mean that poverty and starvation must forever be the lot of mankind unless alleviation is brought by the hydrogen bomb. (D.B.R.)

It is probably true that religion is responsible for our moral code, or at least for a moral code. This moral code had its basis in the Bible but was then formalized by people who wanted to suppress all those things of which they were most afraid.

By some people's standards I suppose that atheists and agnostics might be considered immoral in the eyes of a professed Christian. However, even Christians are not without blemish. They have been guilty of:

1 Torture in the Congo.
2 The condemnation of Dreyfus.
3 Continued support of nuclear warfare.

I could continue this list forever but it seems enough to put them in bad odour from a moral point of view. (D.B.R.)

I am afraid that I do not agree that contemporary events bear out scriptural prophecy except in the sense that virtually anything can be so considered if the inclination to do so exists. My own preference is to look upon theological writings as the slightly historical fantasy world of primitive tribesmen, often savage and sometimes of interest. (D.B.R.)

The whole idea of throwing away your life blindly as an imagined service to Christ is a form of glorifying masochism and of self-abasement before power. It is the same pattern as that of the Russians who made confessions of guilt when prosecuted by Stalin. It is an essentially oriental attitude which Christianity took over when it attributed to God the moral defects of cruel despots. (D.B.R.)

You would be doing a completely wrong act if you abandoned your children in order to practise some spectacular self-sacrifice in a distant country. You should try to bear in mind that there is no reason to believe in Christian doctrines and that much of the Christian ethic is unworthy of self-respecting people. (D.B.R.)

The historical evidence for the existence of Christ the man is flimsy. The views attributed to him are another matter. Such views enable one to assess an individual, hypothetical or existing, who might hold them.

Some of the ethical views which purport to come from him are supportable. The hallucinatory conviction that he possessed divinity was shared by many wandering mystics and lunatics of the day. (D.B.R.)

I think that if there go on being great wars and great oppressions and many people leading very unhappy lives, probably religion will go on, because I've observed that the belief in the goodness of God is inversely proportional to the evidence. When there's no evidence for it at all, people believe it, and when things are going well and you might believe it, they don't. So I think that if people solve their social problems religion will die out. (B.R.S.M.)

I am myself a dissenter from all known religions, and I hope that every kind of religious belief will die out. I regard it as a disease, as belonging to the infancy of human reason, and to a stage of development which we are now outgrowing. Probably no one outside an African Mission now believes that unbaptized children go to hell because Adam ate an apple. (F.T.O.P.)

If you wish to persuade people that because Adam ate an apple, all who have never heard of this interesting occurrence will be roasted in an everlasting fire by a benevolent Deity, you must catch them young, make them stupid by means of drink or drugs, and carefully isolate them from all contact with books or companions capable of making them think. (P.I.C.)

The immense majority of ministers of religion support war whenever it occurs, though in peacetime they are often pacifists. In supporting war, they give emphatic utterance to their conviction that *God* is on their side, and lend religious support to the persecution of men who think wholesale slaughter unwise. (E.S.O.)

Who ever heard of a theologian prefacing his creed, or a politician concluding his speeches, with a statement as to the probable error in his opinions? It is an odd fact that subjective certainty is inversely proportional to objective certainty. The less reason a man has to suppose himself in the right, the more vehemently he asserts that there is no doubt whatever that he is exactly right. It is a practice of theologians to laugh at science because it changes. '*Look* at us,' they say. '*What* we asserted at the *Council of Nicea* we still assert; whereas what scientists asserted only two or three years ago is already forgotten and antiquated.' Men who speak in this way have not grasped the great idea of successive approximations. (E.S.O.)

In Peking, China in 1921 while I was on a lecture tour I suddenly contracted double pneumonia, but in addition to that I had heart disease, kidney disease, dysentery, and phlebitis. My illness provided me with the pleasure of reading my obituary notices, which I had always desired without expecting my wishes to be fulfilled. One missionary paper, I remember, had an obituary notice of one sentence: 'Missionaries may be pardoned for heaving a sigh of relief at the news of Mr Bertrand Russell's death.' I fear they must have heaved a sigh of a different sort when they found that I was not dead after all.

I was told that the Chinese said that they would bury me by the Western Lake and build a shrine to my memory. I have some slight regret that this did not happen, as I might have become a God, which would have been very *chic* for an atheist. (A.B.R. Volume II.)

CHAPTER III

◆◆◆◆◆◆◆◆◆◆◆◆◆◆◆◆◆◆◆◆◆

Sex and Marriage

LORD RUSSELL'S views on sex and marriage were not greeted with any great applause by the multitude, but his name alone brought vindictive and sudden fury when anyone suggested that his views on sex might be *correct*. In spite of the fact that in the second half of the twentieth century the mention of sex became a respectable subject, few philosophers dared to approach it. Somehow sex and sin are still synonymous terms, and until recent years, even scientific investigations into sex were considered wicked and viewed with suspicion and alarm. Lord Russell spent about one per cent of his time dealing with sex, but the general public thought it was 99 per cent.

In 1929 Lord Russell's book, *Marriage and Morals,* upset the faith of a whole generation of post Puritan moralists. Eleven years later this single book set off such a storm of protest that he was legally deprived of a specially created professorship at the City College of New York in 1940. As John Dewey described the situation at the time, in a journal called *The Nation,* 'The persons, if there be such, who go to Bertrand Russell's writings in search of filth and obscenity will be disappointed.' But this statement from America's most renowned philosopher had little effect on the conscience of most Americans. Lord Russell's writings were described as 'pools of blood'. It was further charged that

Lord Russell was, 'the Master mind of free love, of sexual promiscuity for the young and hatred for parents'. One orthodox eminent Divine told his followers that 'any professor guilty of teaching or writing ideas which will multiply the stages upon which these tragedies are set shall not be countenanced in this city'. The news media then reported further charges such as 'quicksand threatened', 'the snake is in the grass', and 'children reared as pawns of a godless state'. One city official even called Lord Russell a 'dog', and further proposed that, 'if we had an adequate system of immigration, that bum could not land within a thousand miles of our shores'. Few people in power paid any attention to Einstein's support when he said, 'Great Spirits have always found violent opposition from mediocrities. The latter cannot understand it when a man does not thoughtlessly submit to hereditary prejudices but honestly and courageously uses his intelligence.' Socrates found himself in similar trouble in the fifth century B.C.

The following official catalogue descriptions of the three specific courses that Lord Russell was supposed to teach at the *City College of New York* do not appear unduly sexual or obscene.

Philosophy 13: A study of modern concepts of logic and its relations to science, mathematics, and philosophy.

Philosophy 24B: A study of the problems in the foundations of mathematics.

Philosophy 27: The relations of pure to applied sciences and the reciprocal influence of metaphysics and scientific theories.

In 1950 when Lord Russell accepted his Nobel Prize, many Americans were shocked. As one theologian put it, 'How could this beast of the human race accept any prize?' It was thought by those imbued with taboo morality that anyone who would write such a book was unfit to teach. Similar reactions occurred elsewhere, and for a time he was subject to an almost complete boycott throughout the United States. Few

books have been subject to such violent controversy.
Part of this controversy stems from the fact that most
people like to think themselves more rational than they
are. If, for example, married persons find themselves
incompatible, the opponents of reason seem to think
that they should go on comfortably thinking themselves
in a state of marital bliss. Lord Russell said this was an
outcome of taboo morality.

There are many who claim that in recent years all
the mortar in the joints has loosened and that the
sexual bars have tumbled down in disgrace. This belief
is totally without foundation. It is true that we no
longer practice prudery and hypocrisy to the extent it
existed in previous ages and that nudity has become less
wicked than it once was, but the subject of sex, however, is still a forbidden subject with no trespassing signs
glowing for anyone to see who would like to discuss the
subject openly among respectable ladies and gentlemen,
not to mention children. It seems that those famous
twins, sex and sin, will remain with us for a long time
to come. In any other field of inquiry 'no trespassing'
signs are curiously absent. Most parents, for instance,
do not show any undue apprehension about their children watching a television programme that deals in
depth on subjects such as 'the psychological causes of
war', 'why we must build a better nuclear *defense
system*', 'the need for a clean bomb', or 'how to figure
your income tax if a clean bomb cannot be developed
in time'. One can only suppose that because these
matters are only trivial it is not necessary to post the
'No Trespassing' signs on these subjects. But alas SEX
is a different matter indeed. Most parents would be horrified if a television programme were created to explore
openly, and frankly, a candid examination of the most
effective techniques in sexual intercourse with live mod-
el demonstrations. Recently it has been charged that
many movies are not fit for public view because nudity,
filth, and our familiar twins, sex and sin, are featured
performers. But this indictment would have never occurred if sex had no twin. However, we probably never
would have had our subsequent troubles if only Adam
had refused the apple. For instance, Catholic apologists

would have us think that their counterattack on sexual freedom has been a smashing success, and that the population dilemma no longer exists. They seem to think that the prospect of seven billion souls on earth in the year 2000 will bring about a sea of tranquillity. Lord Russell thought that this prospect was a tiny bit exaggerated. However, the Curia, the official experts on Sin and Impure Thoughts, continue to perpetuate their special beliefs in face of this self-destructing social dilemma.

As noted earlier in the editor's introduction, Lord Russell's eminence in the intellectual world was firmly established with the publication of the last volume of *Principia Mathematica* in 1913. At this time he was still virtually unknown outside of professional circles. A few years later, however, after his unorthodox views on sex and marriage shocked a whole generation, his name became the most famous in the entire philosophical world—but for the *wrong reasons*. In the 20th century the Victorian fog began to lift, but most societies still regarded sex as a bit wicked. For example, Lord Russell found himself unable to be in entire agreement with those solemn moralists who think that sexual intercourse between a duly married and devout CHRISTIAN COUPLE is wicked if the impulse happens to strike them between 12 and 3 P.M. on GOOD FRIDAY. Every change in dress and sexual attitudes and behaviour was thought to be a decline in standards and a horrible fall from grace. Lord Russell's open views on sexual freedom were bitterly attacked by bigots and obscurantists during his lifetime. However, even his death on February 2, 1970, did not still the voices of some bigots who did not notice that he had indeed died. In regard to the sexual vigour of old people, one lady wrote the following to an American columnist: I wonder if the woman who shamelessly signed herself 'Still Enjoying It' at age 73 is aware that even Bertrand Russell gave up sex at an early age. Ask Bertrand Russell, who will celebrate his 100th birthday next year.' The columnist replied to this charge with the following answer. 'I regret being the bearer of bad news, but Bertrand Russell died on February 2, 1970. He was married four

times. At 63 he married his secretary who was 25. His
fourth marriage took place when he was 80. His bride
was 52. Lord Russell, incidentally, made it to almost
98, which speaks fairly well for sex among the Geritol
set. And those who know say he was a pincher to the
end.'

Many of the selections in this chapter are taken from
his book, *Marriage and Morals,* and show Lord Russell
at his wittiest. The humour displayed on the pages
which follow is not intended, however, to be amusing
for its own sake. 'Naivete' is one thing, wisdom is
another; it is hoped that readers will bear this difference
in mind. This chapter is loaded with delightful surprises
which range from profound satire to hilarious sallies as
Lord Russell emptied his arsenal with massive under-
statement and devastating logic. Unlike some of his
contemporaries he did not consider himself an official
expert on sin. Above all, the reader will see at a glance
that Lord Russell refused to revere sexual taboos
cached in centuries of hoary myths. The morality of
modern Iceland is the supreme example of a relief from
ancient taboos in spite of the fact that it is quite cold
there.

It is odd that neither the Church nor modern public
opinion condemns petting, provided it stops short at a
certain point. At what point sin begins is a matter to
which casuists differ. One eminently orthodox Catholic
divine laid it down that a confessor may fondle a nun's
breasts, provided he does it without evil intent. But I
doubt whether modern authorities would agree with
him on this point. (U.E.)

The phrase 'in the sight of God' puzzles me. One would
suppose that God sees everything, but apparently this is
a mistake. He does not see Reno, for you cannot be
divorced in the sight of God. Register offices are a
doubtful point. I notice that respectable people, who
would not call on anybody who lives in open sin, are
quite willing to call on people who have had only a

civil marriage; so apparently God does see register offices. (U.E.)

Tolstoy and Mahatma Gandhi, in their old age, laid it down that *all* sexual intercourse is wicked, even in marriage and with a view to offspring. The Manicheans thought likewise, relying upon men's native sinfulness to supply them with a continually fresh crop of disciples. This doctrine, however, is heretical, though it is equally heretical to maintain that marriage is as praiseworthy as celibacy. Tolstoy thinks tobacco almost as bad as sex; in one of his novels, a man who is contemplating murder smokes a cigarette first in order to generate the necessary homicidal fury. Tobacco, however, is not prohibited in the Scriptures, though, as Samuel Butler points out, St Paul would no doubt have denounced it if he had known of it. (U.E.)

[According to Saint Thomas] *Divine Law* directs us to love God; also, in a lesser degree, our neighbour. It forbids fornication, because the father should stay with the mother while the children are being reared. It forbids birth control, as being against nature; it does not, however, on this account forbid life-long celibacy. Matrimony should be indissoluble, because the father is needed in the education of the children, both as more rational than the mother, and as having more physical strength when punishment is required. Not all carnal intercourse is sinful, since it is natural; but to think the married state as good as continence is to fall into the heresy of Jovinian. There must be strict monogamy; polygyny is unfair to women, and polyandry makes paternity uncertain. Incest is to be forbidden because it would complicate family life. Against brother-sister incest there is a very curious argument: that if the love of husband and wife were combined with that of brother and sister, mutual attraction would be so strong as to cause unduly frequent intercourse. (H.W.P.)

St Paul's views were emphasized and exaggerated by the early Church; celibacy was considered holy and men retired into the desert to wrestle with Satan while he filled their imaginations with lustful visions. (M.M.)

If the old morality is to be re-established, certain things are essential; some of them are already done, but experience shows that these alone are not effective. The first essential is that the education of girls should be such as to make them stupid and superstitious and ignorant; this requisite is already fulfilled in schools over which the churches have any control. The next requisite is a very severe censorship upon all books giving information on sex subjects; this condition also is coming to be fulfilled in England and in America, since the censorship, without change in the law, is being tightened up by the increasing zeal of the police. These conditions, however, since they exist already, are clearly insufficient. The only thing that will suffice is to remove from young women all opportunity of being alone with men: girls must be forbidden to earn their living by work outside the home; they must never be allowed an outing unless accompanied by their mother or an aunt; the regrettable practice of going to dances without a chaperon must be sternly stamped out. It must be illegal for an unmarried woman under fifty to possess a motor-car, and perhaps it would be wise to subject all unmarried women once a month to medical examination by police doctors, and to send to a penitentiary all such as were found to be not virgins. The use of contraceptives must, of course, be eradicated, and it must be illegal in conversation with unmarried women to throw doubt upon the dogma of eternal damnation. These measures, if carried out vigorously for a hundred years or more, may perhaps do something to stem the rising tide of immorality. I think, however, that in order to avoid the risk of certain abuses, it would be necessary that all policemen and all medical men should be castrated. Perhaps it would be wise to carry this policy a step further, in view of the inherent depravity of the male character. I am inclined to think that moralists would be well advised to advocate that all men should be castrated, with the exception of ministers of religion. Since reading *Elmer Gantry*, I have begun to feel that even this exception is perhaps not quite wise. (M.M.)

Christianity, and more particularly St Paul, introduced an entirely novel view of marriage, that it existed not primarily for the procreation of children, but to prevent the sin of fornication. (I Cor. vii. 1–9.)

St Paul makes no mention whatever of children; the biological purpose of marriage appears to him wholly unimportant. This is quite natural, since he imagined that the Second Coming was imminent and that the world would soon come to an end. At the Second Coming men were to be divided into sheep and goats, and the only thing of real importance was to find oneself among the sheep on that occasion. St Paul holds that sexual intercourse, even in marriage, is something of a handicap in the attempt to win salvation (I Cor. vii. 32–4). Nevertheless it is possible for married people to be saved, but fornication is deadly sin, and the unrepentant fornicator is sure to find himself among the goats. I remember once being advised by a doctor to abandon the practice of smoking, and he said that I should find it easier if, whenever the desire came upon me, I proceeded to suck an acid drop. It is in this spirit that St Paul recommends marriage. He does not suggest that it is quite as pleasant as fornication, but he thinks it may enable the weaker brethren to withstand temptation; he does not suggest for a moment that there may be any positive good in marriage, or that affection between husband and wife may be a beautiful and desirable thing, nor does he take the slightest interest in the family; fornication holds the centre of the stage in his thoughts, and the whole of his sexual ethics is arranged with reference to it. It is just as if one were to maintain that the sole reason for baking bread is to prevent people from stealing cake. (M.M.)

The Puritans, in their determination to avoid the pleasures of sex, became somewhat more conscious than people had been before of the pleasures of the table. As a seventeenth-century critic of Puritanism says:

*Would you enjoy gay nights and pleasant dinners?
Then must you board with saints and bed with
sinners.*

It would seem, therefore, that the Puritans did not
succeed in subduing the purely corporeal part of our
human nature, since what they took away from sex
they added to gluttony. Gluttony is regarded by the
Catholic Church as one of the seven deadly sins, and
those who practise it are placed by Dante in one of the
deeper circles of hell, but it is a somewhat vague sin,
since it is hard to say where a legitimate interest in food
ceases, and guilt begins to be incurred. Is it wicked to
eat anything that is not nourishing? If so, with every
salted almond we risk damnation. (M.M.)

Men have from time immemorial been allowed in practice, if not in theory, to indulge in illicit sexual relations. It has not been expected of a man that he should
be a virgin on entering marriage, and even after marriage, infidelities are not viewed very gravely if they
never come to the knowledge of a man's wife and
neighbours. The possibility of this system has depended
upon prostitution. This institution, however, is one
which it is difficult for a modern to defend, and few
will suggest that women should acquire the same rights
as men through the establishment of a class of male
prostitutes for the satisfaction of women who wish, like
their husbands, to seem virtuous without being so. Every conventional moralist who takes the trouble to
think it out will see that he is committed in practice to
what is called the double standard, that is to say, the
view that sexual virtue is more essential in a woman
than in a man. It is all very well to argue that his
theoretical ethic demands continence of men also. To
this there is the obvious retort that the demand cannot be enforced on the men since it is easy for
them to sin secretly. The conventional moralist is
thus committed against his will not only to an inequali-
ty as between men and women, but also to the view
that it is better for a young man to have intercourse
with prostitutes than with girls of his own class, in spite

of the fact that with the latter, though not with the former, his relations are not mercenary, and may be affectionate and altogether delightful. Moralists, of course, do not think out the consequences of advocating a morality which they know will not be obeyed; they think that so long as they do not advocate prostitution they are not responsible for the fact that prostitution is the inevitable outcome of their teaching. This, however, is only another illustration of the well-known fact that the professional moralist in our day is a man of less than average intelligence. (M.M.)

The Catholic Church has not remained so unbiological as St Paul and the hermits of the Thebaid. From St Paul one gathers that marriage is to be regarded solely as a more or less legitimate outlet for lust. One would not gather from his words that he would have any objection to birth control: on the contrary, one would be led to suppose that he would regard as dangerous the periods of continence involved in pregnancy and childbirth. The Church has taken a different view. Marriage in the orthodox Christian doctrine has two purposes: one, that recognized by St Paul, the other, the procreation of children. The consequence has been to make sexual morality even more difficult than it was made by St Paul. Not only is sexual intercourse only legitimate within marriage, but even between husband and wife it becomes a sin unless it is hoped that it will lead to pregnancy. The desire for legitimate offspring is, in fact, according to the Catholic Church, the only motive which can justify sexual intercourse. But this motive always justifies it, no matter what cruelty may accompany it. If the wife hates sexual intercourse, if she is likely to die of another pregnancy, if the child is likely to be diseased or insane, if there is not enough money to prevent the utmost extreme of misery, that does not prevent the man from being justified in insisting on his conjugal rights, provided only that he hopes to beget a child. (M.M.)

The view of the orthodox moralist (this includes the police and the magistrates, but hardly any modern educators) on the question of sex knowledge may, I fancy, be fairly stated as follows. There is no doubt that sexual misconduct is promoted by sexual thoughts, and that the best road to virtue is to keep the young occupied in mind and body with matters wholly unconnected with sex. They must, therefore, be told nothing whatever about sex; they must as far as possible be prevented from talking about it with each other, and grown-ups must pretend that there is no such topic. It is possible by these means to keep a girl in ignorance until the night of her marriage, when it is to be expected that the facts will so shock her as to produce exactly that attitude towards sex which every sound moralist considers desirable in women. (M.M.)

Catholic teaching has a two-fold basis; it rests, on the one hand, upon the asceticism which we already find in St Paul, on the other, upon the view that it is good to bring into the world as many souls as possible, since every soul is capable of salvation. For some reason which I do not understand, the fact that souls are equally capable of damnation is not taken into account, and yet it seems quite as relevant. Catholics, for example, use their political influence to prevent Protestants from practising birth control, and yet they must hold that the great majority of Protestant children whom their political action causes to exist will endure eternal torment in the next world. This makes their action seem somewhat unkind, but doubtless these are mysteries which the profane cannot hope to understand. (M.M.)

Within the monogamic family there are many varieties. Marriages may be decided by the parties themselves or by their parents. In some countries the bride is purchased; in others, e.g. France, the bridegroom. Then there may be all kinds of differences as regards divorce, from the Catholic extreme, which permits no divorce, to the law of old China, which permitted a man to divorce his wife for being a chatterbox. Constancy or quasi-constancy in sex relations arises among animals, as well as human beings, where, for the preservation of

the species, the participation of the male is necessary
for the rearing of the young. Birds, for example, have
to sit upon their eggs continuously to keep them warm,
and also have to spend a good many hours of the day
getting food. To do this is, among many species, impossible for one bird, and therefore male co-operation is
essential. The consequence is that most birds are mod-
els of virtue. Among human beings the co-operation of
the father is a great biological advantage to the offspring, especially in unsettled times and among turbu-
lent populations; but with the growth of modern civilization the role of the father is being increasingly taken
over by the State, and there is reason to think that a
father may cease before long to be biologically advantageous, at any rate in the wage-earning class. If this
should occur, we must expect a complete breakdown of
traditional morality, since there will no longer be any
reason why a mother should wish the paternity of her
child to be indubitable. Plato would have us go a step
further, and put the State not only in the place of the
father but in that of the mother also. I am not myself
sufficiently an admirer of the State, or sufficiently impressed with the delights of orphan asylums, to be enthusiastic in favour of this scheme. (M.M.)

Malinowski found it quite impossible, in spite of his
best argumentative efforts, to persuade his friends on
the islands that there is such a thing as paternity. They
regarded this as a silly story invented by the missionaries. Christianity is a patriarchal religion, and cannot
be made emotionally or intellectually intelligible to people who do not recognize fatherhood. Instead of 'God
the Father' it would be necessary to speak of 'God the
Maternal Uncle,' but this does not give quite the right
shade of meaning, since fatherhood implies both power
and love, whereas in Melanesia the maternal uncle has
the power and the father has the love. The idea that
men are God's children is one which cannot be con-
veyed to the Trobriand Islanders, since they do not
think that anybody is the child of any male. Consequently missionaries are compelled to tackle first the

facts of physiology before they can go on to preach their religion. One gathers from Malinowski that they have had no success in this initial task, and have, therefore, been quite unable to proceed to the teaching of the Gospel. (M.M.)

Cruelty is in theory a perfectly adequate ground for divorce, but it may be interpreted so as to become absurd. When the most eminent of all film stars was divorced by his wife for cruelty, one of the counts in the proof of cruelty was that he used to bring home friends who talked about Kant. I can hardly suppose that it was the intention of the California legislators to enable any woman to divorce her husband on the ground that he was sometimes guilty of intelligent conversation in her presence. (M.M.)

The need for prostitution arises from the fact that many men are either unmarried or away from their wives on journeys, that such men are not content to remain continent, and that in a conventionally virtuous community they do not find respectable women available. Society therefore sets apart a certain class of women for the satisfaction of those masculine needs which it is ashamed to acknowledge yet afraid to leave wholly unsatisfied. The prostitute has the advantage, not only that she is available at a moment's notice, but that, having no life outside her profession, she can remain hidden without difficulty, and the man who has been with her can return to his wife, his family, and his church with unimpaired dignity. She, however, poor woman, in spite of the undoubted service she performs, in spite of the fact that she safeguards the virtues of wives and daughters and the apparent virtue of church-wardens, is universally despised, thought to be an outcast, and not allowed to associate with ordinary people except in the way of business. This blazing injustice began with the victory of the Christian religion, and has been continued ever since. (M.M.)

Missionaries may argue that the superiority of the Christian code is known by revelation. The philosopher, however, must observe that other religions make the same claim; the Manicheans thought it wicked to eat any animal food except fish, but many sects have considered this exception an abomination. The Dukhobors refused military service, but held it proper to dance naked all together round a camp fire; being persecuted for the former tenet in Russia, they emigrated to Canada, where they were persecuted for the latter. The Mormons had a divine revelation in favour of polygamy, but under pressure from the United States Government they discovered that the revelation was not binding. (H.S.E.P.)

The recognition of children as one of the purposes of marriage is very partial in Catholic doctrine. It exhausts itself in drawing the inference that intercourse not intended to lead to children is sin. It has never gone so far as to permit the dissolution of a marriage on the ground of sterility. However ardently a man may desire children, if it happens that his wife is barren, he has no remedy in Christian ethics. The fact is that the positive purpose of marriage, namely procreation, plays a very subordinate part, and its main purpose remains, as with St Paul, the prevention of sin. Fornication still holds the centre of the stage, and marriage is still regarded essentially as a somewhat less regrettable alternative. (M.M.)

It is permissible with certain precautions to speak in print of *coitus,* but it is not permissible to employ the monosyllabic synonym for this word. This has recently been decided in the case of *Sleeveless Errand*. Sometimes this prohibition of simple language has grave consequences; for example, Mrs Sanger's pamphlet on birth control, which is addressed to working women, was declared obscene on the ground that working women could understand it. Dr Marie Stopes's books, on the other hand, are not illegal, because their language can only be understood by persons with a certain amount of education. The consequence is that, while it is permissible to teach birth control to the well-to-do, it is criminate to teach it to wage-earners and their wives. I commend this fact to the notice of the Eugenic Society, which is perpetually bewailing the fact that wage-earners breed faster than middle-class people, while carefully abstaining from any attempt to change the state of the law which is the cause of this fact. (M.M.)

The commonest objection to birth control is that it is against 'nature'. (For some reason we are not allowed to say that celibacy is against nature; the only reason I can think of is that it is not new.) Malthus saw only three ways of keeping down the population: moral restraint, vice, and misery. Moral restraint, he admitted, was not likely to be practised on a large scale. 'Vice', i.e., birth control, he, as a clergyman, viewed with abhorrence. There remained misery. In his comfortable parsonage, he contemplated the misery of the great majority of mankind with equanimity, and pointed out the fallacies of the reformers who hoped to alleviate it. (U.E.)

Very few men or women who have had a conventional upbringing have learnt to feel decently about sex and marriage. Their education has taught them that deceitfulness and lying are considered virtues by parents and teachers; that sexual relations, even within marriage, are more or less disgusting, and that in propagating the species men are yielding to their animal nature while women are submitting to a painful duty. This attitude has made marriage unsatisfying both to men and women, and the lack of instinctive satisfaction has turned to cruelty masquerading as morality. (M.M.)

A boy should be taught that in no circumstances is conversation on sexual subjects permissible, not even in marriage. This increases the likelihood that when he marries he will give his wife a disgust of sex and thus preserve her from the risk of adultery. Sex outside marriage is sin; sex within marriage is not sin, since it is necessary to the propagation of the human species, but it is a disagreeable duty imposed on man as a punishment for the Fall, and to be undertaken in the same spirit in which one submits to a surgical operation.

Unfortunately, unless great pains are taken, the sexual act tends to be associated with pleasure, but by sufficient moral care this can be prevented, at any rate in the female. It is illegal in England to state in print that a wife can and should derive sexual pleasure from intercourse. (I have myself heard a pamphlet condemned as obscene in a court of law on this among other grounds). It is on the above outlook in regard to sex that the attitude of the law, the Church, and the old-fashioned educators of the young is based. (M.M.)

Sex relations as a dignified, rational, wholehearted activity in which the complete personality co-operates, do not often, I think, occur in America outside marriage. To this extent the moralists have been successful. They have not prevented fornication; on the contrary, if anything, their opposition, by making it spicy, has made it more common. But they have succeeded in making it almost as undesirable as they say it is, just as they have succeeded in making much of the alcohol consumed as poisonous as they assert all alcohol to be. They have compelled young people to take sex neat, divorced from daily companionship, from a common work, and from all psychological intimacy. The more timid of the young do not go so far as complete sexual relations, but content themselves with producing prolonged states of sexual excitement without satisfaction, which are nervously debilitating, and calculated to make the full enjoyment of sex at a later date difficult or impossible. (M.M.)

Most men and women, given suitable conditions, will feel passionate love at some period of their lives. For the inexperienced, however, it is very difficult to distinguish passionate love from mere sex hunger; especially is this the case with well-brought-up girls, who have been taught that they could not possibly like to kiss a man unless they loved him. If a girl is expected to be a virgin when she marries, it will very often happen that she is trapped by a transient and trivial sex attraction, which a woman with sexual experience could easily distinguish from love. This has undoubtedly been a frequent cause of unhappy marriages. Even where mutual love exists, it may be poisoned by the belief of one or both that it is sinful. This belief may, of course, be well founded. Parnell, for example, undoubtedly sinned in committing adultery, since he thereby postponed the fulfillment of the hopes of Ireland for many years. (M.M.)

Peasant children early become accustomed to what are called the facts of life, which they can observe not only among human beings but among animals. They are thus saved from both ignorance and fastidiousness. The carefully educated children of the well-to-do, on the contrary, are shielded from all practical knowledge of sexual matters, and even the most modern parents, who teach children out of books, do not give them that sense of practical familiarity which the peasant child acquires. The triumph of Christian teaching is when a man and woman marry without either having had previous sexual experience. (M.M.)

In the present day when the human race is falling, I find that eminent divines think that it is much more important to prevent artificial insemination than it is to prevent the kind of world war that will exterminate the whole lot of us. (B.R.S.M.)

Christ tells us to become as little children, but little children cannot understand the differential calculus, or the principles of currency, or the modern methods of combating disease. To acquire such knowledge is no part of our duty, according to the church. The church no longer contends that knowledge is in itself sinful, though it did so in its palmy days; but the acquisition of knowledge, even though not sinful, is dangerous, since it may lead to pride of intellect, and hence to a questioning of the Christian dogma. Take, for example, two men, one of whom has stamped out yellow fever throughout some large region in the tropics but has in the course of his labours had occasional relations with women to whom he was not married; while the other has been lazy and shiftless, begetting a child a year until his wife died of exhaustion and taking so little care of his children that half of them died from preventable causes, but never indulging in illicit sexual intercourse. Every good Christian must maintain that the second of these men is more virtuous than the first. (W.N.C.)

CHAPTER IV

✦✦✦✦✦✦✦✦✦✦✦✦✦✦✦✦✦✦

Education

ALTHOUGH Lord Russell's contributions to education have not been as titanic or promethean as his contributions to mathematics and philosophy, the impact of his views on education were considerable. He was an ardent leader of those who held that education ought to emphasize scientifc methods of inquiry rather than the transmission of a settled body of knowledge. He refused to compromise with those who adopted persecution, censorship, and other controls over education.

Lord Russell had wide personal experience with a variety of educational problems. From 1927 to 1932 he and his wife, Dora Winifred Black, directed the activities of an experimental school for young children. Since 1900 he lectured widely in England, America, and the Far East at such notable institutions as Cambridge University, England; the University of Chicago, the University of California, and Harvard University in the United States; and the National University in Peking, China. He was also prevented from accepting a number of other professional engagements because he advocated 'dangerous' ideas. He was called an enemy of reason and morality by those who prefer that educators *instill* eternal creeds, instead of a spirit of scientific inquiry.

During the present century considerable attention has been focused upon the more desirable values of education—the developing of scientific attitudes and the forming of mental habits which lead to sound judgments. To these, however, much as enlightened educators may regret it, most students react with indifference. What they really value from the education to which they are exposed are final *answers* to questions. The thought that objective methods of inquiry are more valid than fixed answers rarely occurs to the stereotyped mind. What is needed in education are not systems of dogma, but rather an attitude of scientific inquiry. Students ought to be taught to base their beliefs upon observation and inference as impersonal and as much devoid of dogmatic bias as is possible for human beings.

In Western culture nudity is curious indeed. Young people are taught that the body must be covered, but which parts have puzzled moralists. For example, who can imagine a saint with his hands covered? Which parts of the body are wicked and which ones less wicked? Bertrand Russell held that the idea that nudity is wicked depends upon which culture one is in and which parts ought to be covered. Before Christian missionaries invited themselves to explore the morals of African tribes, women's breasts were not considered sinful to gaze upon. With the advent of Christian missionaries, the Africans were taught that some parts of the body are wicked to show in public. This clearly shows that sin and wickedness is culturally relative.

The flashes of wit that Lord Russell displays in the selections which follow point up the struggle between those who advocate inflexible doctrines and those who advocate freedom in education. The former are largely responsible for planting seeds of fear, hate, and intolerance in the minds of the young which often blossom into full-scale persecution crusades. History records numerous instances of the dreadful consequences of this kind of education. Hitler's Germany is a case in point. There are other undesirable results of this educational method. Science, for example, remained static until a few brave men challenged the opinions of ancient authorities. Before 1500 anyone who dared disagree with the official opinion of the Church or State was silenced.

It is only in a spirit of free inquiry that desirable

learning can take place. In this kind of atmosphere students are not compelled to believe in tenets, but only in evidence which is objective. The substitution of evidence for dogma, as a basis for belief, is one of the great achievements that science has conferred upon mankind. Lord Russell refused to surrender to the pressures of those who insisted upon less than a scientific attitude in education. He paid the price in 1940 in New York for his candid views.

Lord Russell held that peace can never be permanently secured until the education of children is changed. Warlike heroes such as Nelson, Wellington, Napoleon, Pershing, Eisenhower should not be glorified. Lord Russell gave the following advice to those who teach history. 'In the teaching of history there should be no undue emphasis upon one's own country. The history of wars should be a small part of what is taught. There will be, after all, plenty of opportunity for adventure, even dangerous adventure. Boys can go to the antarctic for their Holidays and young men can go to the moon'. Let us look at some illustrations of what ought not to be taught in school.

Man, it would seem, has descended from arboreal apes. They lived a happy life in tropical forests, eating coconuts when they were hungry, and throwing them at each other when they were not. They were perpetually occupied in gymnastics, and acquired an agility which, to us, is truly astonishing. But after some millions of years of this arboreal paradise, their numbers increased to the point where the supply of coconuts was no longer adequate. The population problem set in, and was dealt with in two different ways: those who lived in the middle of the forest learned to throw coconuts with such accuracy as to disable adversaries, whose consequent death relieved the pressure of population, but those who lived on the edge of the forest found another method: they looked out over the fields and discovered that they yielded delicious fruits of various kinds quite as pleasant as coconuts, and gradually they came down from the trees and spent more and more time in the open on the ground. They soon discovered that if you live on the ground it is easy to pick up stones, which are more effective missiles than coconuts. (N.H.C.W.)

I am not myself in any degree ashamed of having changed my opinions. What physicist who was already active in 1900 would dream of boasting that his opinions had not changed during the last half century? In science men change their opinions when new knowledge becomes available, but philosophy in the minds of many is assimilated rather to theology than to science. A theologian proclaims eternal truths, the creeds remain unchanged since the Council of Nicea. Where nobody knows anything, there is no point in changing your mind. (D.M.M.M.)

Owing to the identification of religion with virtue, together with the fact that the most religious men are not the most intelligent, a religious education gives courage to the stupid to resist the authority of educated men, as has happened, for example, where the teaching of evolution has been made illegal. So far as I can remember, there is not one word in the Gospels in praise of intelligence; and in this respect ministers of religion follow gospel authority more closely than in some others. (E.S.O.)

If you think that your belief is based upon reason, you will support it by argument, rather than by persecution, and will abandon it if the argument goes against you. But if your belief is based on faith, you will realize that argument is useless, and will therefore resort to force either in the form of persecution or by stunting and distorting the minds of the young in what is called 'education.' This last is peculiarly dastardly, since it takes advantage of the defencelessness of immature minds. Unfortunately it is practised in a greater or less degree in the schools of every civilized country. (H.S.E.P.)

Punctuality is a quality the need of which is bound up with social co-operation. It has nothing to do with the relation of the soul to God, or with mystic insight, or with any of the matters with which the more elevated and spiritual moralists are concerned. One would be surprised to find a saint getting drunk, but one would not be surprised to find him late for an engagement. And yet in the ordinary business of life punctuality is absolutely necessary. (E.S.O.)

To modern educated people, it seems obvious that matters of fact are to be ascertained by observation, not by consulting ancient authorities. But this is an entirely modern conception, which hardly existed before the seventeenth century. Aristotle maintained that women have fewer teeth than men; although he was twice married, it never occurred to him to verify this statement by examining his wives' mouths. He said also that children would be healthier if conceived when the wind is in the north. One gathers that the two Mrs Aristotles both had to run out and look at the weathercock every evening before going to bed. He states that a man bitten by a mad dog will not go mad, but any other animal will (*Hist. Am.*, 704a); that the bite of the shrewmouse is dangerous to horses, especially if the mouse is pregnant (ibid., 604b); that elephants suffering from insomnia can be cured by rubbing their shoulders with salt, olive oil, and warm water (ibid., 605a); and so on and so on. Nevertheless, classical dons, who have never observed any animal except the cat and the dog, continue to praise Aristotle for his fidelity to observation. (I.S.S.)

It is not altogether true that persuasion is one thing and force is another. Many forms of persuasion—even many of which everybody approves—are really a kind of force. Consider what we do to our children. We do not say to them: 'Some people think the earth is round, and others think it flat; when you grow up, you can, if you like, examine the evidence and form your own conclusion.' Instead of this we say: 'The earth *is* round.' By the time our children are old enough to examine the evidence, our propaganda has closed their minds, and the most persuasive arguments of the Flat Earth Society make no impression. The same applies to the moral precepts that we consider really important, such as 'don't pick your nose' or 'don't eat peas with a knife'. There may, for aught I know, be admirable reasons for eating peas with a knife, but the hypnotic effect of early persuasion has made me completely incapable of appreciating them. (P.:A.N.S.A.)

In universities, mathematics is taught mainly to men who are going to teach mathematics to men who are going to teach mathematics to. . . . Sometimes, it is true, there is an escape from this treadmill. Archimedes used mathematics to kill Romans, Galileo to improve the Grand Duke of Tuscany's artillery, modern physicists (grown more ambitious) to exterminate the human race. It is usually on this account that the study of mathematics is commended to the general public as worthy of State support. (H.S.E.P.)

Until the time of Galileo, astronomers, following Aristotle, believed that everything in the heavens, from the moon upwards, is unchanging and incorruptible. Since Laplace, no reputable astronomer has held this view. Nebulae, stars, and planets, we now believe, have all developed gradually. Some stars, for instance the companion of Sirius, are 'dead'; they have at some time undergone a cataclysm which has enormously diminished the amount of light and heat radiating from them. Our own planet, in which philosophers are apt to take a parochial and excessive interest, was once too hot to support life, and will in time be too cold. After ages during which the earth produced harmless trilobites and butterflies, evolution progressed to the point at which it generated Neros, Genghis Khans, and Hitlers. This, however, is a passing nightmare; in time the earth will become again incapable of supporting life, and peace will return. (U.E.)

Generalizing, we may say that Dr Dewey, like everyone else, divides beliefs into two classes, of which one is good and the other bad. He holds, however, that a belief may be good at one time and bad at another. A belief about some event in the past is to be classified as 'good' or 'bad', not according to whether the event really took place, but according to the future effects of the belief. The results are curious. Suppose somebody says to me: 'Did you have coffee with your breakfast this morning?' If I am an ordinary person, I shall try to remember. But if I am a disciple of Dr Dewey I shall say: 'Wait a while; I must try two experiments before I can tell you.' I shall, then, first make myself believe that I had coffee, and observe the consequences, if any; I shall then make myself believe that I did not have coffee, and again observe the consequences, if any. I shall then compare the two sets of consequences, to see which I found the more satisfactory. If there is a balance on one side I shall decide for that answer. If there is not, I shall have to confess that I cannot answer the question.

But this is not the end of our trouble. How am I to know the consequences of believing that I had coffee for breakfast? If I say 'the consequences are such-and-such,' this in turn will have to be tested by its consequences before I can know whether what I have said was a 'good' or a 'bad' statement. And even if this difficulty were overcome, how am I to judge which set of consequences is the more satisfactory? One decision as to whether I had coffee may fill me with contentment, the other with determination to further the war effort. Each of these may be considered good, but until I have decided which is better I cannot tell whether I had coffee for breakfast. (H.W.P.)

The date of the creation of the world (according to the orthodox view) can be inferred from the genealogies in Genesis, which tell how old each patriarch was when his oldest son was born. Some margin of controversy was permissible, owing to certain ambiguities and to differences between the Septuagint and the Hebrew text; but in the end Protestant Christendom generally accepted the date 4004 B.C., fixed by Archbishop Usher. Dr. Lightfoot, Vice-Chancellor of the University of

Cambridge, who accepted this date for the Creation, thought that a careful study of Genesis made even greater precision possible; the creation of man, according to him, took place at 9.0 a.m. on October 23rd. This, however, has never been an article of faith; you might believe, without risk of heresy, that Adam and Eve came into existence on October 16th or October 30th, provided your reasons were derived from Genesis. The day of the week was, of course, known to have been Friday, since God rested on the Saturday. (R.S.)

The first German to take notice of Hume was Immanuel Kant, who had been content, up to the age of about forty-five, with the dogmatic tradition derived from Leibniz. Then, as he says himself, Hume 'awakened him from his dogmatic slumbers'. After meditating for twelve years, he produced his great work, the *Critique of Pure Reason*; seven years later, at the age of sixty-four, he produced the *Critique of Practical Reason,* in which he resumed his dogmatic slumbers after nearly twenty years of uncomfortable wakefulness. (U.E.)

Children are made to learn bits of Shakespeare by heart, with the result that ever after they associate him with pedantic boredom. If they could meet him in the flesh, full of jollity and ale, they would be astonished, and if they had never heard of him before they might be led by his jollity to see what he had written. But if at school they had been inoculated against him, they will never be able to enjoy him. The same sort of thing applies to music lessons. Human beings have certain capacities for spontaneous enjoyment, but moralists and pedants possess themselves of the apparatus of these enjoyments, and having extracted what they consider the poison of pleasure they leave them dreary and dismal and devoid of everything that gives them value. Shakespeare did not write with a view to boring schoolchildren; he wrote with a view to delighting his audiences. If he does not give you delight, you had better ignore him. (N.H.C.W.)

Fichte laid it down that education should aim at destroying free will, so that, after pupils have left school,
they shall be incapable, throughout the rest of their
lives, of thinking or acting otherwise than as their
schoolmasters would have wished. But in his day this
was an unattainable ideal. What he regarded as the best
system in existence produced Karl Marx. In future such
failures are not likely to occur where there is dictator-
ship. Diet, injections, and injunctions will combine,
from a very early age, to produce the sort of character
and the sort of beliefs that the authorities consider
desirable, and any serious criticism of the powers that
be will become psychologically impossible. Even if all
are miserable, all will believe themselves happy, because the government will tell them that they are
so. (I.S.S.)

Boys and young men acquire readily the moral sentiments of their social milieu, whatever these sentiments
may be. The boy who has been taught at home that it is
wicked to swear, easily loses this belief when he finds
that the schoolfellows whom he most admires are ad-
dicted to blasphemy. (H.S.E.P.)

Dread of disaster makes everybody act in the very way
that increases the disaster. Psychologically the situation
is analogous to that of people trampled to death when
there is a panic in a theatre caused by a cry of 'Fire!' In
the situation that existed in the great depression, things
could only be set right by causing the idle plant to work
again. But everybody felt that to do so was to risk
almost certain loss. Within the framework of classical
economics there was no solution. Roosevelt saved the
situation by bold and heretical action. He spent billions
of public money and created a huge public debt, but by
so doing he revived production and brought his country
out of the depression. Businessmen, who in spite of
such a sharp lesson continued to believe in old-
fashioned economics, were infinitely shocked, and although Roosevelt saved them from ruin, they continued
to curse him and to speak of him as 'the madman in the
White House.' Except for Fabre's investigation of the

behaviour of insects, I do not know any equally striking example of inability to learn from experience. (N.H.C.W.)

You may, if you are an old-fashioned schoolmaster, wish to consider yourself full of universal benevolence, and at the same time derive great pleasure from caning boys. In order to reconcile these two desires you have to persuade yourself that caning has a reformatory influence. If a psychiatrist tells you that it has no influence on some peculiarly irritating class of young sinners, you will fly into a rage and accuse him of being coldly intellectual. There is a splendid example of this pattern in the furious diatribe of the great Dr Arnold of Rugby against those who thought ill of flogging. (H.S.E.P.)

Until very recently, it was universally believed that men are congenitally more intelligent than women; even so enlightened a man as Spinoza decides against votes for women on this ground. Among white men, it is held that white men are by nature superior to men of other colours, and especially to black men; in Japan, on the contrary, it is thought that yellow is the best colour. In Haiti, when they make statues of Christ and Satan, they make Christ black and Satan white. Aristotle and Plato considered Greeks so innately superior to barbarians that slavery is justified so long as the master is Greek and the slave barbarian. (U.E.)

Male superiority in former days was easily demonstrated, because if a woman questioned her husband's he could beat her. From superiority in this respect others were thought to follow. Men were more reasonable than women, more inventive, less swayed by their emotions, and so on. Anatomists, until the women had the vote, developed a number of ingenious arguments from the study of the brain to show that men's intellectual capacities must be greater than women's. Each of these arguments in turn was proved to be fallacious, but it always gave place to another form which the same conclusion would follow. It used to be held that the male foetus acquires a soul after six weeks, but the female only after three months. This opinion also has been abandoned since women have had the vote. Thomas Aquinas states parenthetically, as something entirely obvious, that men are more rational than women. For my part, I see no evidence of this. (U.E.)

Some 'advanced Thinkers' are of opinion that anyone who differs from the conventional opinion must be in the right. This is a delusion; if it were not, truth would be easier to come by than it is. There are infinite possibilities of error, and more cranks take up unfashionable errors than unfashionable truths. I met once an electrical engineer whose first words to me were: 'How do you do? There are two methods of faith-healing, the one practised by Christ and the one practised by most Christian Scientists. I practise the method practised by Christ.' Shortly afterwards, he was sent to prison for making out fraudulent balance-sheets. The law does not look kindly on the intrusion of faith into this region. (U.E.)

I knew an eminent lunacy doctor who took to philosophy, and taught a new logic which, as he frankly confessed, he had learned from his lunatics. When he died he left a will founding a professorship for the teaching of his new scientific methods, but unfortunately he left no assets. Arithmetic proved recalcitrant to lunatic logic. On one occasion a man came to ask me to recommend some of my books, as he was interested in philosophy. I did so, but he returned next day saying that he had been reading one of them, and had found only one statement he could understand, and that one seemed to him false. I asked him what it was, and he said it was the statement that Julius Caesar is dead. When I asked him why he did not agree, he drew himself up and said: 'Because I am Julius Caesar.' (U.E.)

The demand for certainty is one which is natural to man, but is nevertheless an intellectual vice. If you take your children for a picnic on a doubtful day, they will demand a dogmatic answer as to whether it will be fine or wet, and be disappointed in you when you cannot be sure. The same sort of assurance is demanded, in later life, of those who undertake to lead populations into the Promised Land. 'Liquidate the capitalists and the survivors will enjoy eternal bliss.' 'Exterminate the Jews and everyone will be virtuous.' 'Kill the Croats and let the Serbs reign.' 'Kill the Serbs and let the Croats reign.' These are samples of the slogans that have won wide popular acceptance in our time. Even a modicum of philosophy would make it impossible to accept such bloodthirsty nonsense. But so long as men are not trained to withhold judgment in the absence of evidence, they will be led astray by cocksure prophets, and it is likely that their leaders will be either ignorant fanatics or dishonest charlatans. To endure uncertainty is difficult, but so are most of the other virtues. For the learning of every virtue there is an appropriate discipline, and for the learning of suspended judgment the best discipline is philosophy. (U.E.)

Those who have a passion for quick returns and for an exact balance sheet of effort and reward may feel impatient of a study which cannot, in the present state of our knowledge, arrive at certainties, and which encourages what may be thought the time-wasting occupation of inconclusive meditation on insoluble problems. To this view I cannot in any degree subscribe. Some kind of philosophy is a necessity to all but the most thoughtless, and in the absence of knowledge it is almost sure to be a silly philosophy. The result of this is that the human race becomes divided into rival groups of fanatics, each group firmly persuaded that its own brand of nonsense is sacred truth, while the other side's is damnable heresy. Arians and Catholics, Crusaders and Moslems, Protestants and adherents of the Pope, Communists and Fascists, have filled large parts of the last 1,600 years with futile strife, when a little philosophy would have shown both sides in all these disputes that neither had any good reason to believe itself in the right. (U.E.)

When the journey from means to end is not too long, the means themselves are enjoyed if the end is ardently desired. A boy will toil uphill with a toboggan for the sake of a few brief moments of bliss during the descent; no one has to urge him to be industrious, and however he may puff and pant he is still happy. But if instead of the immediate reward you promised him an old-age pension at seventy, his energy would very quickly flag. (A.I.)

Herd pressure is to be judged by two things: first, its intensity, and second, its direction. If it is very intense, it produces adults who are timid and conventional, except in a few rare instances. This is regrettable, however excellent may be the moral standards by which the herd is actuated. In *Tom Brown's Schooldays* there is a boy who is kicked for saying his prayers. This book had a great effect, and among my contemporaries I knew one who had been kicked at school for *not* saying his prayers. I regret to say that he remained through life a prominent atheist. (E.S.O.)

Dr Arnold, the hero of *Tom Brown's Schooldays*, and the admired reformer of public schools, came across some cranks who thought it a mistake to flog boys. Anyone reading his outburst of furious indignation against this opinion will be forced to the conclusion that he enjoyed inflicting floggings, and did not wish to be deprived of this pleasure. (U.E.)

Men of science are being increasingly compelled to pursue the ends of governments rather than those proper to science. The scientist who discovers how to injure others is therefore at least as much honoured as the one who shows us how to benefit ourselves. The pursuit of knowledge for its own sake, which was once the purpose of science, is lost sight of; there are even philosophers who tell us that there is no such thing. A physicist who wishes to study uranium can have access to any amount of public money, but if he wished to devote equal skill and equal labour to the study of (say) carbon, he would have to persuade his government that he was on the track of a method of inventing robots. (B.D.)

In the welter of conflicting fanaticisms, one of the few unifying forces is scientific truthfulness, by which I mean the habit of basing our beliefs upon observations and inferences as impersonal, and as much divested of local and temperamental bias as is possible for human beings. To have insisted upon the introduction of this virtue into philosophy, and to have invented a powerful method by which it can be rendered fruitful, are the chief merits of the philosophical school of which I am a member. The habit of careful veracity acquired in the practise of this philosophical method can be extended to the whole sphere of human activity, producing, wherever it exists, a lessening of fanaticism with an increasing capacity of sympathy and mutual understanding. (H.W.P.)

I was a solitary, shy, priggish youth. I had no experience of the social pleasures of boyhood and did not miss them. But I liked mathematics, and mathematics was suspect because it has no ethical content. I came also to disagree with the theological opinions of my family, and as I grew up I became increasingly interested in philosophy, of which they profoundly disapproved. Every time the subject came up they repeated with unfailing regularity, 'What is mind? No matter. What is matter? Never mind.' After some fifty or sixty repetitions, this remark ceased to amuse me. (P.F.M.)

I think the first thing that led me toward philosophy (though at that time the word 'philosophy' was still unknown to me) occurred at the age of eleven. My childhood was mainly solitary as my only brother was seven years older than I was. No doubt as a result of so much solitude I became rather solemn, with a great deal of time for thinking but not much knowledge for my thoughtfulness to exercise itself upon. I had, though I was not yet aware of it, the pleasure in demonstrations which is typical of the mathematical mind. After I grew up I found others who felt as I did on this matter.

My friend G. H. Hardy, who was professor of pure mathematics, enjoyed this pleasure in a very high degree. He told me once that if he could find a proof that I was going to die in five minutes he would of course be sorry to lose me, but this sorrow would be quite outweighed by pleasure in the proof. I entirely sympathized with him and was not at all offended. Before I began the study of geometry somebody had told me that it proved things and this caused me to feel delight when my brother said he would teach it to me. Geometry in those days was still 'Euclid'. My brother began at the beginning with the definitions. These I accepted readily enough. But he came next to the axioms. 'These', he said, 'can't be proved, but they have to be assumed before the rest can be proved.' At these words my hopes crumbled. I had thought it would be wonderful to find something that one could *prove*, and then it turned out that this could only be done by means of assumptions of which there was no proof. I looked at my brother with a sort of indignation and said: 'But why should I admit these things if they can't be proved?' He replied, 'Well, if you won't, we can't go on.' (P.F.M.)

There are some simple maxims which I think might be commended to writers of expository prose. First: never use a long word if a short word will do. Second: if you want to make a statement with a great many qualifications, put some of the qualifications in separate sentences. Third: do not let the beginning of your sentence lead the reader to an expectation which is contradicted by the end. Take, say, such a sentence as the following, which might occur in a work on sociology: 'Human beings are completely exempt from undesirable behaviour patterns only when certain prerequisites, not satisfied except in a small percentage of actual cases, have, through some fortuitous concourse of favourable circumstances, whether congenital or environmental, chanced to combine in producing an individual in whom many factors deviate from the norm in a socially advantageous manner.' Let us see if we can translate this sentence into English. I suggest the following: 'All men are scoundrels, or at any rate almost all. The men who are not must have had unusual luck, both in their birth and in their upbringing.' This is shorter and more intelligible, and says just the same thing. But I am afraid any professor who used the second sentence instead of the first would get the sack.

This suggests a word of advice to such of my readers as may happen to be professors. I am allowed to use plain English because everybody knows that I could use mathematical logic if I chose. Take the statement: 'Some people marry their deceased wives' sisters.' I can express this in language which only becomes intelligible after years of study, and this gives me freedom. I suggest to young professors that their first work should be written in a jargon only to be understood by the erudite few. With that behind them, they can ever after say what they have to say in a language 'understanded of the people'. In these days, when our very lives are at the mercy of the professors, I cannot but think that they would deserve our gratitude if they adopted my advice. (P.F.M.)

Oppenheimer was disgraced and prevented from pursuing his work largely because he doubted the practicability of the hydrogen bomb at a time when this doubt was entirely rational. The F.B.I., which has only the level of education to be expected among policemen, considers itself competent to withhold visas from the most learned men in Europe on grounds which every person capable of understanding the matters at issue knows to be absurd. This evil has reached such a point that international conferences of learned men in the United States have become impossible. (P.F.M.)

Those who advocate common usage in philosophy sometimes speak in a manner that suggests the *mystique* of the 'common man'. They may admit that in organic chemistry there is need of long words, and that quantum physics requires formulas that are difficult to translate into ordinary English, but philosophy (they think) is different. It is not the function of philosophy— so they maintain—to teach something that uneducated people do not know; on the contrary, its function is to teach superior persons that they are not as superior as they thought they were, and those who are *really* superior can show their skill by making sense of common sense.

No one wants to alter the language of common sense, any more than we wish to give up talking of the sun rising and setting. But astronomers find a different language better, and I contend that a different language is better in philosophy.

Let us take an example, that of perception. There is here an admixture of philosophical and scientific questions, but this admixture is inevitable in many questions, or, if not inevitable, can only be avoided by confining ourselves to comparatively unimportant aspects of the matter in hand.

Here is a series of questions and answers.

Q. When I see a table, will what I see be still there if I shut my eyes?

A. That depends upon the sense in which you use the word 'see'.

Q. What is still there when I shut my eyes?

A. This is an empirical question. Don't bother me with it, but ask the physicists.

Q. What exists when my eyes are open, but not when they are shut?

A. This again is empirical, but in deference to previous philosophers I will answer you: coloured surfaces.

Q. May I infer that there are two senses of 'see'? In the first, when I 'see' a table, I 'see' something conjectural about which physics has vague notions that are probably wrong. In the second, I 'see' coloured surfaces which cease to exist when I shut my eyes.

A. That is correct if you want to think clearly, but our philosophy makes clear thinking unnecessary. By oscillating between the two meanings, we avoid paradox and shock, which is more than most philosophers do. (P.F.M.)

I think there ought to be no rules whatever prohibiting improper publications. I think that partly because if there are rules stupid magistrates will condemn really valuable work because it happens to shock them. Another reason is that I think prohibitions immensely increase people's interest in pornography, as in anything else. I used often to go to America during Prohibition, and there was far more drunkenness than there was before, and I think that prohibition of pornography has much the same effect. The following illustration will amply suffice. The philosopher Empedocles thought it was very very wicked to munch laurel leaves, and he laments that he will have to spend ten thousand years in outer darkness because he munched laurel leaves. Now nobody has ever told me to munch laurel leaves and I have never done it, but Empedocles who was told not to, did it. And I think the same applies to pornography. Suppose, for instance, filthy post cards were permitted. I think for the first year or two there would be a great demand for them, and then people would get bored and nobody would look at them again. (B.R.S.M.)

The modern parent wants his children to be unconstrained in his presence as in his absence; he wants them to feel pleasure when they see him coming; he does not want a fictitious Sabbath Calm while he is watching, succeeded by pandemonium as soon as he turns his back. (E.E.E.C.)

The prevention of free inquiry is unavoidable so long as the purpose of education is to produce belief rather than thought, to compel the young to hold positive opinions on doubtful matters rather than to let them see the doubtfulness and be encouraged to independence of mind. Education ought to foster the wish for truth, not the conviction that some particular creed is the truth. (P.S.R.)

In the immense majority of children, there is the raw material of a good citizen, and also the raw material of a criminal. Scientific psychology shows that flogging on weekdays and sermons on Sundays do not constitute the ideal technique for the production of virtue. (E.E.E.C.)

Physical punishment I believe to be never right. In mild forms it does little harm, though no good; in severe forms, I am convinced that it generates cruelty and brutality. It is true that it often produces no resentment against the person who inflicts it; where it is customary, boys adapt themselves to it and expect it as part of the course of nature. But it accustoms them to the idea that it may be right and proper to inflict physical pain for the purpose of maintaining authority—a peculiarly dangerous lesson to teach to those who are likely to acquire positions of power. (E.E.C.)

Scientific method, although in its more refined forms it may seem complicated, is in essence remarkably simple. It consists in observing such facts as will enable the observer to discover general laws governing facts of the kind in question. A scientific opinion is one which there is some reason to believe true; an unscientific opinion is one which is held for some reason other than its probable truth. When a man tells you that he knows the exact truth about anything, you are safe in inferring that he is an inexact man. (T.S.O.)

Philosophical progress seems to me analogous to the gradually increasing clarity of outline of a mountain approached through mist, which is vaguely visible at first, but even at last remains in some degree indistinct. What I have never been able to accept is that the mist itself conveys valuable elements of truth. There are those who think that clarity, because it is difficult and rare, should be suspect. The rejection of this view has been the deepest impulse in all my philosophical work. (B.W.B.R. Preface.)

I should not wish to be thought in earnest only when I am solemn. There are many things that seem to me important to be said, but not best said in a portentous tone of voice. Indeed, it has become increasing evident to me that portentousness is often, though not always, a device for warding off too close scrutiny. I cannot believe in 'sacred' truths. Whatever one may believe to be true, one ought to be able to convey without any apparatus of Sunday sanctification. (B.W.B.R. Preface.)

On a very great many matters my views since I began to write on philosophy have undergone repeated changes. In philosophy, though not in science, there are those who make such changes a matter of reproach. This, I think, results from the tradition which assimilates philosophy with theology rather than with science. For my part, I should regard an unchanging system of philosophical doctrines as proof of intellectual stagnation. (B.W.B.R. Preface.)

CHAPTER V

◆◆◆◆◆◆◆◆◆◆◆◆◆◆◆◆◆◆

Politics

ALTOGETHER Lord Russell had extensive experience with politics and with the effects of politics. His activities ranged from membership in the House of Lords to serving two terms in prison for failing to agree with those in power on war policy.

During World War I he wrote a pamphlet in protest against the sentencing of a conscientious objector; for this he was fined one hundred pounds. A few months after this incident he was sentenced to six months' imprisonment for quoting the report of a congressional investigation into the use of federal troops against strikers. His pacifistic views crystallized when he said that neither the Allies nor the Central Powers could solve any problem by means of war. He changed his opinion, however, in the late thirties when Hitler and Mussolini made their totalitarian motives clear. During World War II he was a vigorous supporter of the free nations in the West. Since his visit to Russia in 1920 he has been a consistent opponent of communism in both theory and practice.

With the advent of the atomic age a new question arose: Is victory possible for either side in a nuclear contest? In the summer of 1955 he summoned news reporters from around the globe to listen to a last-minute appeal from a number of scientists regarding the possible effects of a war conducted with nuclear weapons. On July 9, 1955, just prior to the summit meeting of the Big Four nations in Geneva, he met the press to report the opinion of some of the most eminent scientists of our time on this grave problem. As Lord Russell phrased it, 'shall we put an end to the human race?' These scientists signed the following resolution: 'In view of the fact that in any future war nuclear weapons will certainly be employed, and that such weapons threaten the continued existence of mankind, we urge the Governments of the world to realize, and to acknowledge publicly, that their purposes cannot be furthered by a world war, and we urge them, consequently, to find peaceful means for the settlement of all matters of dispute among them.' This resolution was the outcome of a previous conference between Lord Russell and Albert Einstein in which they decided a public appeal must be made to focus attention on the problem of human survival in a modern war. The resolution was written by Lord Russell and signed by Einstein and nine other Nobel Prize winners in Science. This was Einstein's final word to humanity; he died the very day Lord Russell received a letter from him confirming his agreement to this plea.

On September 11, 1961, Lord Russell was again sentenced to Brixton Prison. On this occasion he was charged with another failure to agree with those in power. He said, 'I will not pretend to obey a government which is organizing the massacre of the whole of mankind.' Later on the next day, September 12, 1961, he said, 'It was only step by step and with great reluctance that we were driven to non-violent civil disobedience.' On this second occasion Lord and Lady Russell were both sentenced and served several actual days in Brixton Prison before being released for 'good behaviour'. This protest by the committee of one hundred in Trafalgar Square that Lord Russell led in 1961 was the first major street demonstration by a man of world renown on the issue of mankind's survival, but how long this warning to governments can endure is the supreme dilemma.

Lord Russell was firmly convinced that the fear of nuclear war and the imminent daily and hourly risk of the end of the human race are products of human folly, not decrees of fate. They are not, as many people suppose, results of man's inherent warlike nature. During the Cuban missile crisis and the Sino-Indian dispute in 1962, Lord Russell once again reaffirmed his basic belief that a nuclear war would leave nothing to be desired by civilization. In his book, *Unarmed Victory*, he said that 'within a brief period of time, there would cease to be any to enjoy the poetry of Shakespeare, the music of Bach or Mozart, or the genius of Plato or Newton'.

The kind of political structure Lord Russell hoped to see was one in which power is apportioned with more intelligence than it has been in the past. In his opinion the central problem of political theory is: 'how to combine that degree of individual initiative which is necessary for progress, with the degree of social cohesion which is necessary for survival'. The history of Western civilization has not been too encouraging in this respect, but mankind now has at its disposal weapons of sudden universal extinction, which may cause men to review their motives with grave concern. War, it seems, has now become a sport. For instance, on nationwide television, in an interview in March 1971, General Maxwell Taylor likens War to a 'ball game' in which tactics to be employed will be dependent upon the 'progress' in the game. The General also reminds us that we ought not to 'judge an *actor* before the final curtain is down'. This assessment of the sport of War is curious indeed. One of the troubles about the merits of war is that neither adversary is particularly keen about admitting a defeat at the end of the contest. As Lord Russell pointed out, 'Vanity is a motive of Immense potency.' The emotional impulse to 'get the better of one's opponent' has not ceased since the dawn of what historians often refer to as *Civilization*. Lord Russell was convinced that debates on human survival in the Nuclear Age ought to be conducted by rational adversaries with a sense of history and a compassion for the continued existence of the species *Man*.

The problems involved in international power politics in a scientific society are, without doubt, the most serious men have had to face thus far. It is now imperative that men settle their political differences by some method other than war. Lord Russell held that a society, such as we have at present, in which thought and technique are scientific, can be stable, given certain conditions. The minimum prerequisite conditions for peace are: a single government of the world with a monopoly of police power, a general diffusion of wealth so that no nation has special cause for envy, a low birth-rate throughout the world, and an atmosphere in which individual initiative in science, art, and play can thrive. Lord Russell knew that the world is a long way from achieving these noble objectives, but he held that men could achieve them if they seriously chose to adopt them.

When Lord Russell was asked if he could envision the world in the twenty-first century he said: 'This is an impossible question. I rule it out. I do not know at all. I do think that once the knowledge of nuclear capabilities becomes general there will always be the threat of a nuclear war. The nuclear peril represents a danger which is likely to last as long as governments possess nuclear weapons, and perhaps longer if such destructive objects get into private hands.' In the final volume of his autobiography he said: 'Like Cassandra, I am doomed to prophesy evil and not be believed. Her promises came true. I desperately hope that mine will not.'

The wisdom that Lord Russell displays in the selections in this chapter is somewhat paradoxical. He was a very serious critic of politics and political theory but he was also one of the sharpest satirists of this century. Most social critics fail to hold the interest of the reader because their style of writing is 'dry'. The reader who has gone this far will have discovered that Lord Russell's style is anything but dull.

I am persuaded that there is absolutely no limit in the absurdities that can, by government action, come to be generally believed. Give me an adequate army, with power to provide it with more pay and better food than falls to the lot of the average man, and I will undertake, within thirty years, to make the majority of the population believe that two and two are three, that water freezes when it gets hot and boils when it gets cold, or any other nonsense that might seem to serve the interest of the State. Of course, even when these beliefs had been generated, people would not put the kettle in the refrigerator when they wanted it to boil. That cold makes water boil would be a Sunday truth, sacred and mystical, to be professed in awed tones, but not to be acted on in daily life. What would happen would be that any verbal denial of the mystic doctrine would be made illegal, and obstinate heretics would be 'frozen' at the stake. No person who did not enthusiastically accept the official doctrine would be allowed to teach or to have any position of power. Only the very highest officials, in their cups, would whisper to each other what rubbish it all is; then they would laugh and drink again. (U.E.)

There are some desires which, though very powerful, have not, as a rule, any great *political* importance. Most men at some period of their lives desire to marry, but as a rule they can satisfy this desire without having to take any political action. There are, of course, exceptions; the rape of the Sabine women is a case in point. (N.P.A.S.)

When the British Government very unwisely allowed the Kaiser to be present at a naval review at Spithead, the thought which arose in his mind was not the one which we had intended. What he thought was: 'I must have a navy as good as Grandmama's.' And from this thought have sprung all our subsequent troubles. The world would be a happier place if acquisitiveness were always stronger than rivalry. But in fact, a great many men will cheerfully face impoverishment if they can thereby secure complete ruin for their rivals. Hence the present level of the income tax. (N.P.A.S.)

If politics is to become scientific, and if the event is not to be constantly surprising, it is imperative that our political thinking should penetrate more deeply into the springs of human action. What is the influence of hunger upon slogans? How does their effectiveness fluctuate with the number of calories in your diet? If one man offers you democracy and another offers you a bag of grain, at what stage of starvation will you prefer the grain to the vote? (N.P.A.S.)

One of the troubles about vanity is that it grows with what it feeds on. The more you are talked about, the more you will wish to be talked about. The condemned murderer, I am told—I have had no personal experience—who is allowed to see the account of his trial in the Press is indignant if he finds a newspaper which has reported it inadequately. And the more he finds about himself in other newspapers, the more indignant he will be with the one whose reports are meagre. Politicians and literary men are in the same case. And the more famous they become, the more difficult the press cutting agency finds it to satisfy them. It is scarcely possible to exaggerate the influence of vanity throughout the range of human life, from the child of three to the potentate at whose frown the world trembles. Mankind have even committed the impiety of attributing similar desires to the Deity, whom they imagine avid for continual praise. (N.P.A.S.)

Most political leaders acquire their position by causing large numbers of people to believe that these leaders are actuated by altruistic desires. It is well understood that such a belief is more readily accepted under the influence of excitement. Brass bands, mob oratory, lynching, and war are stages in the development of the excitement. I suppose the advocates of unreason think that there is a better chance of profitably deceiving the populace if they keep it in a state of effervescence. Perhaps it is my dislike of this sort of process which leads people to say that I am unduly rational. (H.S.E.P.)

The increase of organization has brought into existence new positions of power. Everybody has to have executive officials, in whom, at any moment, its power is concentrated. It is true that officials are usually subject to control, but the control may be slow and distant. From the young lady who sells stamps in a post office all the way up to the Prime Minister, every official is invested, for the time being, with some part of the power of the State. You can complain of the young lady if her manners are bad, and you can vote against the Prime Minister at the next election if you disapprove of his policy. But both the young lady and the Prime Minister can have a very considerable run for their money before (if ever) your discontent has any effect. This increase in the power of officials is a constant source of irritation to everybody else. In most countries they are much less polite than in England; the police, especially in America for instance, seem to think you must be a rare exception if you are not a criminal. This tyranny of officials is one of the worst results of increasing organization, and one against which it is of the utmost importance to find safeguards if a scientific society is not to be intolerable to all but an insolent aristocracy of Jacks-in-office. (I.S.S.)

Politics is largely governed by sententious platitudes which are devoid of truth. One of the most widespread popular maxims is, 'Human nature cannot be changed.' No one can say whether this is true or not without first defining 'human nature'. But as used it is certainly false. When Mr A utters the maxim, with an air of portentous and conclusive wisdom, what he means is that all men everywhere will always continue to behave as they do in his own home town. A little anthropology will dispel this belief. Among the Tibetans, one wife has many husbands, because men are too poor to support a whole wife; yet family life, according to travellers, is no more unhappy than elsewhere. The practice of lending one's wife to a guest is very common among uncivilized tribes. The Australian aborigines, at puberty, undergo a very painful operation which, throughout the rest of their lives greatly diminishes sexual potency. Infanticide, which might seem contrary to human nature, was almost universal before the rise of Christianity, and is recommended by Plato to prevent over-population. Private property is not recognized among some savage tribes. Even among highly civilized people, economic considerations will override what is called 'human nature'. (U.E.)

The conscientious Radical is faced with great difficulties. He knows he can increase his popularity by being false to his creed, and appealing to hatreds that have nothing to do with the reforms in which he believes. For example: a community that suffers from Japanese competition can easily be made indignant about bad labour conditions in Japan, and the unfair price-cutting that they render possible. But if the speaker goes on to say that it is Japanese *employers* who should be opposed, not Japanese *employees*, he will lose a large part of the sympathy of his audience. The Radical's only ultimate protection against demagogic appeals to misguided hatreds lies in education: he must convince intellectually a sufficient number of people to form the nucleus of a propagandist army. This is undoubtedly a difficult task, while the whole force of the State and the plutocracy is devoted to the fostering of unreason. But it is perhaps not so hopeless a task as many are now inclined to believe; and in any case it cannot be shirked, since the appeal to unreasoning emotion can always be better done by charlatans. (C.S.)

I cannot be content with a brief moment of riotous living followed by destitution, and however clever the scientists may be, there are some things that they cannot be expected to achieve. When they have used up all the easily available sources of energy that nature has scattered carelessly over the surface of our planet, they will have to resort to more laborious processes, and these will involve a gradual lowering of the standard of living. Modern industrialists are like men who have come for the first time upon fertile virgin land, and can live for a little while in great comfort with only a modicum of labour. It would be irrational to hope that the present heyday of industrialism will not develop far beyond its present level, but sooner or later, owing to the exhaustion of raw material, its capacity to supply human needs will diminish, not suddenly, but gradually. This could, of course, be prevented if men exercised any restraint or foresight in their present frenzied exploitation. Perhaps before it is too late they will learn to do so. (N.H.C.W.)

How long will it be before the accessible oil in the world is exhausted? Will all the arable land be turned into dust-bowls as it has been in large parts of the United States? Will the population increase to the point where men again, like their remote ancestors, have no leisure to think of anything but the food supply? Such questions are not to be decided by general philosophical reflections. Communists think that there will be plenty of oil; if there are no capitalists. Some religious people think that there will be plenty of food if we trust in Providence. Such ideas are superficial, even when they are called scientific, as they are by the Communists. (N.H.C.W.)

We all know that the price of food goes up, but most of us attribute this to the wickedness of the Government. If we live under a progressive Government, it makes us reactionary; if we live under a reactionary Government, it turns us into Socialists. Both these reactions are superficial and frivolous. All Governments, whatever their political complexion, are at present willy-nilly in the grip of natural forces which can only be dealt with by a degree of intelligence of which mankind hitherto has shown little evidence. (N.H.C.W.)

I do not think any reasonable person can doubt that in India, China, and Japan, if the knowledge of birth-control existed, the birth-rate would fall very rapidly. In Africa the process might take longer, but there also it could be fairly easily achieved if Negro doctors, trained in the West, were given the funds to establish medical clinics in which every kind of medical information would be given. I do not suppose that America would contribute to this beneficent work, because if either party favoured it, that party would lose the Catholic vote in New York State, and therefore the Presidency. This obviously would be a greater disaster than the extermination of the human race by atomic war. (N.H.C.W.)

Some opponents of Communism are attempting to produce an ideology for the Atlantic Powers, and for this purpose they have invented what they call 'Western Values'. These are supposed to consist of toleration, respect for individual liberty, and brotherly love. I am afraid this view is grossly unhistorical. If we compare Europe with other continents, it is marked out as the persecuting continent. Persecution only ceased after long and bitter experience of its futility; it continued as long as either Protestants or Catholics had any hope of exterminating the opposite party. The European record in this respect is far blacker than that of the Mohammedans, the Indians or the Chinese. No, if the West can claim superiority in anything, it is not in moral values but in science and scientific technique. (N.H.C.W.)

Everything done by European administrators to improve the lot of Africans is, at present, totally and utterly futile because of the growth of population. The Africans, not unnaturally, though now mistakenly, attribute their destitution to their exploitation by the white man. If they achieve freedom suddenly before they have men trained in administration and a habit of responsibility, such civilization as white men have brought to Africa will quickly disappear. It is no use for doctrinaire liberals to deny this; there is a standing proof in the island of Haiti. (N.H.C.W.)

If two hitherto rival football teams, under the influence of brotherly love, decided to co-operate in placing the football first beyond one goal and then beyond the other, no one's happiness would be increased. There is no reason why the zest derived from competition should be confined to athletics. Emulation between teams or localities or organizations can be a useful incentive. But if competition is not to become ruthless and harmful, the penalty for failure must not be disaster, as in war, or starvation, as in unregulated economic competition, but only loss of glory. Football would not be a desirable sport if defeated teams were put to death or left to starve. (A.I.)

In a shipwreck the crew obey orders without the need of reasoning with themselves, because they have a common purpose which is not remote, and the means to its realization are not difficult to understand. But if the Captain were obliged like the Government, to explain the principles of currency in order to prove his commands wise, the ship would sink before his lecture was finished. (A.I.)

The savage, in spite of his membership of a small community, lived a life in which his initiative was not too much hampered by the community. The things that he wanted to do, usually hunting and war, were also the things that his neighbours wanted to do, and if he felt an inclination to become a medicine man he only had to ingratiate himself with some individual already eminent in that profession, and so, in due course, to succeed to his powers of magic. If he was a man of exceptional talent, he might invent some improvement in weapons, or a new skill in hunting. These would not put him into any opposition to the community, but, on the contrary, would be welcomed. The modern man lives a very different life. If he sings in the street he will be thought to be drunk and if he dances a policeman will reprove him for impeding the traffic. (A.I.)

Two great religions—Buddhism and Christianity—have sought to extend to the whole human race the co-operative feeling that is spontaneous towards fellow tribesmen. They have preached the brotherhood of man, showing by the use of the word 'brotherhood' that they are attempting to extend beyond its natural bounds an emotional attitude which, in its origin, is biological. If we are all children of God, then we are all one family. But in practice those who in theory adopted this creed have always felt that those who did not adopt it were not children of God but children of Satan, and the old mechanism of hatred of those outside the tribe has returned, giving added vigour to the creed, but in a direction which diverted it from its original purpose. Religion, morality, economic self-interest, the mere pursuit of biological survival, all supply to our intelligence unanswerable arguments in favour of world-wide cooperation, but the old instincts that have come down to us from our tribal ancestors rise up in indignation, feeling that life would lose its savour if there were no one to hate, that anyone who could love such a scoundrel as So-and-so would be a worm, that struggle is the law of life, and that in a world where we all loved one another there would be nothing to live for. (A.I.)

Before World War I one of the objections commonly urged against votes for women was that women would tend to be pacifists. During the war they gave a large-scale refutation of this charge, and the vote was given to them for their share in the bloody work. (M.M.)

There are many points of view from which the life of man may be considered. There are those who think of him primarily in cultural terms as being capable of lofty art and sublime speculation and discovery of the hidden secrets of nature. There are those who think of him as one of those kinds of animals that are capable of government, though in this respect he is completely outshone by ants and bees. There are those who think of him as the master of war; these include all the men in all countries who decide upon the adornment of public squares, where it is an invariable rule obeyed by all right-thinking public authorities that the most delectable object to be seen by the passers-by is a man on horseback, who is commemorated for his skill in homicide. (N.H.C.W.)

Organizations are of two kinds, those which aim at getting something done, and those which aim at preventing something from being done. The Post Office is an example of the first kind; a fire brigade is an example of the second kind. Neither of these arouses much controversy, because no one objects to letters being carried, and incendiaries dare not avow a desire to see buildings burnt down. But when what is to be prevented is something done by human beings, not by Nature, the matter is otherwise. The armed forces of one's own nation exist—so each nation asserts—to PREVENT aggression by other nations. But the armed forces of other nations exist—or so many people believe—to PROMOTE aggression. If you say anything against the armed forces of your own country, you are a traitor, wishing to see your fatherland ground under the heel of a brutal conqueror. If, on the other hand, you defend a potential enemy State for thinking armed forces necessary to its safety, you malign your own country, whose unalterable devotion to peace only perverse malice could lead you to question. I heard all this said about Germany by a thoroughly virtuous German lady in 1936, in the course of a panegyric on Hitler. (I.S.S.)

I do not pretend that birth control is the only way in which population can be kept from increasing. There are others, which, one must suppose, opponents of birth control would prefer. War has hitherto been disappointing in this respect, but perhaps bacteriological war may prove more effective. If a Black Death could be spread throughout the world once in every generation survivors could procreate freely without making the world too full. There would be nothing in this to offend the consciences of the devout or to restrain the ambitions of nationalists. The state of affairs might be somewhat unpleasant, but what of that? Really high-minded people are indifferent to happiness, especially other people's. (I.S.S.)

In superstitious moments I am tempted to believe in the myth of the Tower of Babel, and to suppose that in our own day a similar but greater impiety is about to be visited by a more tragic and terrible punishment. Perhaps—so I sometimes allow myself to fancy—God does not intend us to understand the mechanism by which He regulates the material universe. Perhaps the nuclear physicists have come so near to the ultimate secrets that

He thinks it time to bring their activities to a stop. And what simpler method could He devise than to let them carry their ingenuity to the point where they exterminate the human race? If I could think that deer and squirrels, nightingales and larks, would survive, I might view this catastrophe with some equanimity, since man has not shown himself worthy to be the lord of creation. But it is to be feared that the dreadful alchemy of the atomic bomb will destroy all forms of life equally, and that the earth will remain forever a dead clod senselessly whirling round a futile sun. I do not know the immediate precipitating cause of this interesting occurrence. Perhaps it will be a dispute about Persian oil, perhaps a disagreement as to Chinese trade, perhaps a quarrel between Jews and Mohammedans for the control of Palestine. Any patriotic person can see that these issues are of such importance as to make the extermination of mankind preferable to cowardly conciliation. (U.E.)

Men, quite ordinary men, will compel children to look on while their mothers are raped. In pursuit of political aims men will submit their opponents to long years of unspeakable anguish. We know what the Nazis did to the Jews at Auschwitz. In mass cruelty, the expulsions of Germans ordered by the Russians fall not very short of the atrocities perpetrated by the Nazis. And how about our noble selves? We would not do such deeds. Oh no! But we enjoy our juicy steaks and our hot rolls while German children die of hunger because our governments dare not face our indignation if they asked us to forgo some part of our pleasures. If there were a Last Judgment as Christians believe, how do you think our excuses would sound before that final tribunal? (U.E.)

Stalin could neither understand nor respect the point of view which led Churchill to allow himself to be peaceably dispossessed as a result of a popular vote. I am a firm believer in democratic representative government as the best form for those who have the tolerance and self-restraint that is required to make it workable. But its advocates make a mistake if they suppose that it can be at once introduced into countries where the average citizen has hitherto lacked all training in the give-and-take that it requires. In a Balkan country, not so many years ago, a party which had been beaten by a narrow margin in a general election retrieved its fortunes by shooting a sufficient number of the representatives of the other side to give it a majority. People in the West thought this characteristic of the Balkans, forgetting that Cromwell and Robespierre had acted likewise. (U.E.)

The American legislators who made the immigration laws consider the Nordics superior to Slavs or Latins or any other white men. But the Nazis, under the stress of war, were led to the conclusion that there are hardly any true Nordics outside Germany; the Norwegians, except Quisling and his few followers, had been corrupted by intermixture with Finns and Lapps and such. Thus politics are a clue to descent. The biologically pure Nordics love Hitler, and if you did not love Hitler, that was proof of tainted blood. (U.E.)

Very little remains of institutions and ways of life that when I was a child appeared as indestructible as granite. I grew up in an atmosphere impregnated with tradition. My parents died before I can remember, and I was brought up by my grandparents. I was taught a kind of theoretic republicanism which was prepared to tolerate a monarch so long as he recognized that he was an employee of the people and subject to dismissal if he proved unsatisfactory. My grandfather, who was no respecter of persons, used to explain this point of view to Queen Victoria, and she was not altogether sympathetic. She did, however, give him the house in Richmond Park in which I spent all my youth. I imbibed certain political principles and expectations, and have on the whole retained the former in spite of being compelled to reject the latter. There was to be ordered progress throughout the world, no revolutions, a gradual cessation of war, and an extension of parliamentary government to all those unfortunate regions which did not yet enjoy it. My grandmother used to laugh about a conversation she had had with the Russian Ambassador. She said to him, 'Perhaps some day you will have a parliament in Russia,' and he replied, 'God forbid, my dear Lady John.' The Russian Ambassador of today might give the same answer if he changed the first word. (P.F.M.)

Neither misery nor folly seems to me any part of the inevitable lot of man. And I am convinced that intelligence, patience, and eloquence can, sooner or later, lead the human race out of its self-imposed tortures provided it does not exterminate itself meanwhile.

On the basis of this belief, I have had always a certain degree of optimism, although, as I have grown older, the optimism has grown more sober and the happy issue more distant. But I remain completely incapable of agreeing with those who accept fatalistically the view that man is born to trouble. The causes of unhappiness in the past and in the present are not difficult to ascertain. There have been poverty, pestilence, and famine, which were due to man's inadequate mastery of nature. There have been wars, oppressions and tortures which have been due to men's hostility to their fellow men. And there have been morbid miseries fostered by gloomy creeds, which have led men into profound inner discords that made all outward prosperity of no avail. All these are unnecessary. In regard to all of them, means are known by which they can be overcome. In the modern world, if communities are unhappy, it is because they choose to be so. Or, to speak more precisely, because they have ignorances, habits, beliefs, and passions, which are dearer to them than happiness or even life. I find many men in our dangerous age who seem to be in love with misery and death, and who grow angry when hopes are suggested to them. (P.F.M.)

At first I imagined that the task of awakening people to the dangers of the Nuclear Peril should not be very difficult. I shared the general belief that the motive of self-preservation is a very powerful one which, when it comes into operation, generally overrides all others. I thought that people would not like the prospect of being fried with their families and their neighbours and every living person that they had heard of. I thought it would only be necessary to make the danger known and that, when this had been done, men of all parties would unite to restore previous safety. I found that this is a mistake. There is a motive which is stronger than self-preservation: it is the desire to get the better of the other fellow. (A.B.R. Volume III.)

Before I went to Russia I imagined that I was going to see an interesting experiment in a new form of representative government. I did see an interesting experiment, but not in representative government. (T.P.T.B.)

I have found that military men think that Christian belief is very important in the contest with Eastern powers, and they think that if you are not a Christian you will not be so vigorous about it. Well, I read the Sermon on the Mount over again and I could not find a word in it to encourage the H-bomb—not a word. (B.R.S.M.)

Worry comes from not facing unpleasant possibilities. A great many people enjoy a *War* provided it is not in their neighbourhood and not too bad. If your head is cut off it immensely diminishes your thinking power. (B.R.S.M.)

I see future possibilities—gloomy ones and hopeful ones—but I think for purposes of definition we had better support gloom. I think that if the human race does not wipe itself out in a final nuclear contest, the greatest danger that I see is regimentation. I think it is quite possible that under the influence of scientific discoveries and administrative possibilities and organization, the world may get so organized that there will be no fun to be had anywhere. (B.R.S.M.)

I think it is possible for communism and capitalism to learn to live side by side in the world together. It is only a question of getting used to each other. Now take the Christians and Mohammedans; they fought each other for about six centuries, during which neither side got any advantage over the other, and at the end of that time some man of genius said: '*Look*, why should not we stop fighting each other and make friends?' Of course, we cannot wait six centuries because there will not be any of us left after six centuries of conflict such as the Mohammedans and Christians had. (B.R.S.M.)

I have heard all the statements pretending that from the newest nuclear bomb there is no fall-out. All these statements are deliberate lies. I had a broadcast discussion on this point and one of the chief governmental nuclear authorities in the U.S. boasted that he had discovered how to make 'clean' bombs and that his research towards this end had been dictated by humanitarian motives. I said, 'Then I suppose you have told the Russians about it?' He replied with horror, 'No, that would be illegal!' Was I to conclude that it was only Russian lives that he wished to spare, not American? (D.B.R.)

I have always considered these hymns typical of Christian pacifism:

> Christian, dost thou see them on the holy ground,
> How the troops of Midian prowl and prowl around?
> Christian, up and smite them, counting gain not loss;
> Smite them by the merit of the Holy Cross.

> The Son of God goes forth to war,
> A Kingly crown to gain;
> His blood-red banners stream afar,
> Who follows in His train?

(D.B.R.)

It is despairing to observe how high-placed men, who in other repects are not devoid of intelligence, can believe, both in the East and the West, that peace is to be preserved by one's own side being always stronger than the other side. It may well be that the next war will end with the stronger side still possessing H-bombs, but neither side possessing live human beings. (F.F.)

In 1997, if we still exist, we must expect rival parties of Russian Commisars and American Marines to travel at enormous expense to the surface of Mars and to keep themselves alive there for a few days while they search for each other. When they find each other, they will exterminate each other. Each side will hear of the extermination of the other side and will proclaim a public holiday to celebrate the glorious victory. (H.M.F.)

CHAPTER VI

◆◆◆◆◆◆◆◆◆◆◆◆◆◆◆◆◆◆

Ethics

INTRODUCTION

THE kind of morality that Lord Russell proposed was one devoid of superstition and organized madness; one where those familiar twins, fear and hate, were absent, and one where men love each other as passionately as they now desire the misery of their enemies. Though it would seem that reasonable men everywhere would rejoice at such a proposal, mankind has thought otherwise and prefers to continue to imitate his barbaric past. As the selections in this chapter will amply reveal, Lord Russell shaved the nonsense from a great variety of popular myths and left each one naked with no place to hide. Consider, for example, the question of voluntary euthanasia. Are civilized men seriously expected to believe that, 'A wise, omnipotent and beneficient *Being* finds so much pleasure in watching the slow agonies of an innocent person that *He* will be angry with those who shorten the ordeal?' It is this sort of sardonic attack on traditional morality that gives the illustrations in this book that unmistakable Russell touch.

For after all, it was not Lord Russell's historic contributions to logic and mathematics that made his writing a joy to read. His works in logic and mathematics can be comprehended only by readers with prerequisite highly technical knowledge in these subjects, and, if

Lord Russell would have published exclusively in these areas, he would have had few readers anywhere. Indeed, it was the pointedness of his wit that made Lord Russell the most widely read philosopher of the twentieth century. When this editor wished to include some sections from Lord Russell's *Principia Mathematica* in his book *The Basic Writings of Bertrand Russell,* Lord Russell replied that the inclusion of more than a few summary pages would 'greatly lessen the sales of your book'. The editor is glad that he accepted Lord Russell's advice. When Lord Russell was 38 years old, he finally decided to write on subjects that could be read by the general public, and much of his writing since 1910 dealt with enormous social problems but he used language that could be, as he said, 'understanded by the people'. As the reader finishes the last word in this book, it should be clear that Lord Russell's social satires made man remember his follies much as a mirror reminds people of the way they really look. He wrote with brilliance and the echo of his words will remain for centuries. Like Socrates, Lord Russell reminded man to question and look a little further and continue the search for truth. Two thousand years seems like a long time, but, as Lord Russell said, 'truth is a long and difficult business and we should not be dogmatic.' Lord Russell received a number of offers to visit purgatory, but, he thought that since Socrates declined similar offers, he should not accept them either.

Throughout history the evolution of man into a self-respecting and undebasing individual has been retarded by ethical and religious beliefs. The genius of Galileo, for example, was challenged by the Holy See on the grounds that what he thought he saw in his telescope was wicked and would have a corrupting influence on church scholars, and might possibly test their faith. There are many who still think that the retrograde influence of religion has declined to such an extent that it no longer poses any threat to cultural and scientific progress, but this view is apparently a mistake.

The recent and sudden expansion of Islam makes this religion of six hundred million rival in numerical strength the Roman Catholic Church. In both cases ancient myths and taboos are revered as eternal truths. The creeds of both groups remain as static as they were when they were invented. Some of the beliefs are absurd. The fundamental creed of Islam, for example, is that all sins can be forgiven provided there is sufficient debasement demonstrated by the penitent. However, there is one curious exception and that is the unforgivable *sin* of doubt concerning the omnipotence, omniscience, and beneficence of *Allah*. For some unexplained reason this special *sin* is not tolerated and can never be forgiven. As Lord Russell pointed out in the Preface to his book, *Why I Am Not a Christian*, 'I think all the great religions of the world—Buddhism, Hinduism, Christianity, Islam, Communism—are both untrue and harmful.' As a matter of simple logic not more than one of them can be true. But the most disquieting effect of this harm is to the unfettered intelligence. After all, Darwin still suffers from the pangs of purgatory because he published his *Origin of Species* in 1859. 'Religion,' as Lord Russell described its effects, has not only done 'untold harm' but has been in constant battle with the spirit of scientific inquiry.

Lord Russell was persuaded that history is against those who think that the threat of the H-bomb, or some other more serious weapons, will make men forget their silly quarrels. After all as Lord Russell noted it was 'Nobel who invented the Nobel Peace Prize and he was a very keen advocator of peace, but he was also the inventor of dynamite'. In solemn moments of contemplation over this horrible discovery, Nobel thought that dynamite would prevent war. Unfortunately, his hopes were never realized.

Lord Russell was perplexed by the morality of governments that seem to find little difficulty in raising enormous sums for the purpose of killing people, but find it a tiresome, and somewhat taxing experience, to appropriate a few pinhead sums for the purpose of killing disease. He was even more horrified at the adoration accorded statues of men commemorated for their special skill in homicide. Lord Russell raised some other interesting questions. Suppose that man's diabolical genius reduced the planet to a mere brother and sister. Should they permit the species to perish, or, could incest be forgiven on this special occasion. As Lord Russell pointed out, 'sin' is not a useful notion, because where 'sin' begins is a doubtful question. Empedocles thought that it was wicked to munch laurel leaves. For some curious reason nudity also seems to change with the seasons. At what specific point sin begins has never been settled by the official experts. If only Empedocles had satisfied his insatiable appetite, we might be prepared to move on to more serious questions.

Throughout the long history of Western philosophy there have been a number of philosophers who demonstrated a special talent for making ethical questions cloudy. Lord Russell thought this unnecessary. He was convinced that the mist surrounding philosophical issues ought not to be admired as droplets of wisdom, because the mist itself conveys no elements of truth whatever. When he was asked to compare science and philosophy on a live unrehearsed BBC television interview his response was audacious, lucid, and candid: 'Science', he said, 'is what we know and philosophy is what we do not know'. But, he added wryly, 'That is a simple definition but no two philosophers would agree.' Lord Russell had little patience with philosophers who made mist their business. He said, 'There are those who think that clarity because it is difficult and rare, should be suspect.' He summarized his philosophy when he said, 'The rejection of this view has been the deepest impulse in all my philosophical work.'

When Lord Russell approached his 93rd birthday, a reporter asked him how he felt and he said, 'Splendid, I live almost entirely on liquids as I have to be most careful about solid food. Things stick in my throat from trying to swallow the pronouncements of politicians. In World War I King George V took the pledge because he thought he could save money, but he used the money to kill Germans. So I drank.' When Lord Russell was asked if his opponents were correct in thinking that he had a habit of changing his mind he said, 'My views have changed in harmony with changes in the world.' Probably his best advice was that, 'We should say stop hating each other. Learn to co-operate. Learn to have international institutions that really work and take what steps you can to world government. That is what I would like to see. That is what I expect.' World government seems like a fantastic dream, but unless this dream can come true all other dreams will have become a useless mist.

As we approach the last quarter of the twentieth century, man has gone to the brink of committing his species and all life on this tiny planet to total annihilation. Man must learn to tolerate his neighbours or perish in a few moments of universal folly. This question—'shall we put an end to the human race'—was the final problem he raised. Lord Russell spent almost a century trying to understand the world, and as he said, 'The business of a philosopher is not to change the world but to understand it.' This Grecian thought was put into a simple, yet timeless formula by Lord Russell when he wrote, 'the *good life* is one inspired by love and guided by wisdom'.

Perhaps the most distinguishing mark of a great thinker is his foresight to see the inevitable before it happens, to see what lesser minds cannot vision. Soon after World War II it became clear to Lord Russell and other eminent scientists that it was their supreme *Moral duty* to warn the world of the impending danger of universal death on our planet unless something were done to prevent the nuclear arms race from spreading any farther. Politicians and statesmen tended to ignore these warnings as well as the masses of civilization. Nevertheless, today even the man in the street is beginning to realize for the first time the gravity of this problem. It is a tribute to Lord Russell that he organized the first protests to help prevent the dread peril. Lord Russell, like Einstein, gave his last moments of reflection to the ethical questions raised by the march of scientific power.

Measures of sterilization should, in my opinion, be very definitely confined to persons who are *mentally* defective. I cannot favour laws such as that of Idaho, which allows sterilization of 'mental defectives, epileptics, habitual criminals, moral degenerates, and sex perverts'. The last two categories here are very vague, and will be determined differently in different communities. The law of Idaho would have justified the sterilization of Socrates, Plato, Julius Caesar, and St Paul. (M.M.)

In addition to the general argument against faith, there is something peculiarly odious in the contention that the principles of the Sermon on the Mount are to be adopted with a view to making nuclear bombs more effective. If I were a Christian, I should consider this the absolute extreme of blasphemy. (H.S.E.P.)

If throughout your life you abstain from murder, theft, fornication, perjury, blasphemy, and disrespect towards your parents, your Church, and your king, you are conventionally held to deserve moral admiration even if you have never done a single kind or generous or useful action. This very inadequate notion of virtue is an outcome of taboo morality, and has done untold harm. (H.S.E.P.)

The Russian Government appears to think that Soviet decrees can change the laws of genetics; the Vatican apparently believes that ecclesiastical decrees could secure adequate nourishment for us all, even if there were only standing room on the planet. Such opinions, to my mind, represent a form of insane megalomania entirely alien to the scientific spirit. (N.C.H.W.)

Christ said 'Thou shalt love thy neighbour as thyself,' and when asked 'who is thy neighbour?' went on to the parable of the Good Samaritan. If you wish to understand this parable as it was understood by His hearers, you should substitute 'German' or 'Japanese' for 'Samaritan.' I fear many present-day Christians would resent such a substitution, because it would compel them to realize how far they have departed from the teaching of the Founder of their religion. (U.E.)

Suppose atomic bombs had reduced the population of the world to one brother and sister; should they let the human race die out? I do not know the answer, but I do not think it can be in the affirmative merely on the ground that incest is wicked. (H.S.E.P.)

The whole conception of 'sin' is one I find very puzzling, doubtless owing to my sinful nature. If 'sin' consisted in causing needless suffering, I could understand, but on the contrary, sin often consists in avoiding needless suffering. Some years ago, in the English House of Lords, a bill was introduced to legalize euthanasia in cases of painful and incurable disease. The patient's consent was to be necessary, as well as several medical certificates. To me, in my simplicity, it would seem natural to require the patient's consent, but the late Archbishop of Canterbury, the English official expert on sin, explained the erroneousness of such a view. The patient's consent turns euthanasia into suicide, and suicide is sin. Their Lordships listened to the voice of authority and rejected the bill. Consequently, to please the Archbishop—and his God, if he reports truly— victims of cancer still have to endure months of wholly useless agony, unless their doctors or nurses are sufficiently humane to risk a charge of murder. I find difficulty in the conception of a God who gets pleasure from contemplating such tortures; and if there were a God capable of such wanton cruelty, I should certainly not think Him worthy of worship. But that only proves how sunk I am in moral depravity. (U.E.)

Has civilization taught us to be more friendly towards one another? The answer is easy. Robins (the English, not the American species) peck an elderly robin to death, whereas men (the English, not the American species) give an elderly man an old-age pension. Within the herd we are more friendly to each other than are many species of animals, but in our attitude towards those outside the herd, in spite of all that has been done by moralists and religious teachers, our emotions are as ferocious as those of any animal, and our intelligence enables us to give them a scope which is denied to even the most savage beast. It may be hoped, though not very confidently, that the more humane attitude will in time come to prevail, but so far the omens are not very propitious. (U.E.)

There is in Aristotle an almost complete absence of what may be called benevolence or philanthropy. The sufferings of mankind, in so far as he is aware of them, do not move him emotionally; he holds them intellectually to be an evil, but there is no evidence that they cause him unhappiness except when the sufferers happen to be his friends. (H.W.P.)

Most stern moralists are in the habit of thinking of pleasure as only of the senses, and, when they eschew the pleasures of sense, they do not notice that the pleasures of power, which to men of their temperament are far more attractive, have not been brought within the ban of their ascetic self-denial. It is the prevalence of this type of psychology in forceful men which has made the notion of sin so popular, since it combines so perfectly humility towards heaven with self-assertion here on earth. The concept of sin has not the hold upon men's imaginations that it had in the Middle Ages, but still dominates the thoughts of many clergymen, magistrates and schoolmasters. When the great Dr Arnold walked on the shores of Lake Como, it was not the beauty of the scene that occupied his thoughts. He meditated, so he tells us, on moral evil. I rather fear that it was the moral evil of school-boys rather than school-masters that produced his melancholy reflections. However that may be, he was led to the unshakable belief that it is good for boys to be flogged. One of the great rewards that a belief in sin has always offered to the virtuous is the opportunity which it affords of inflicting pain without compunction. (H.S.E.P.)

One of the 'grand' conceptions which have proved scientifically useless is the soul. I do not mean that there is positive evidence showing that men have no soul; I only mean that the soul, if it exists, plays no part in any discoverable causal law. There are all kinds of experimental methods of determining how men and animals behave under various circumstances. You can put rats in mazes and men in barbed wire cages, and observe their methods of escape. You can administer drugs and observe their effect. You can turn a male rat into a female, though so far nothing analogous has been done with human beings, even at Buchenwald. It appears that socially undesirable conduct can be dealt with by medical means, or by creating a better environment, and the conception of sin has thus come to seem quite unscientific, except, of course, as applied to the Nazis. There is real hope that, by getting to understand the science of human behaviour, governments may be even more able than they are at present to turn mankind into rabbles of mutually ferocious lunatics. (U.E.)

Cotton goods, after the industry became scientific, could find a market in India and Africa: this was a stimulus to British Imperialism. Africans had to be taught that nudity is wicked; this was done very cheaply by missionaries. In addition to cotton goods we exported tuberculosis and syphilis, but for them there was no charge. (I.S.S.)

As soon as we abandon our own reason, and are content to rely upon authority, there is no end to our trouble. Whose authority? The Old Testament? The New Testament? The Koran? In practice, people choose the book considered sacred by the community in which they are born, and out of that book they choose the parts they like, ignoring the others. At one time, the most influential text in the Bible was: 'Thou shalt not suffer a witch to live.' Nowadays, people pass over this text, in silence if possible; if not, with an apology. And so, even when we have a sacred book, we still choose as truth whatever suits our own prejudices. No Catholic, for instance, takes seriously the text which says that a Bishop should be the husband of one wife. (U.E.)

Consider how much brutality has been justified by the rhyme:

> A dog, a wife, and a walnut tree,
> The more you beat them the better they be.

I have no experience of the moral effect of flagellation on walnut trees, but no civilized person would now justify the rhyme as regards wives. The reformative effect of punishment is a belief that dies hard, chiefly, I think, because it is so satisfying to our sadistic impulses. (U.E.)

I had at one time a very bad fever of which I almost died. In my fever I had a long consistent delirium. I dreamt that I was in Hell, and that Hell is a place full of all those happenings that are improbable but not impossible. The effects of this are curious. Some of the damned, when they first arrive below, imagine that they will beguile the tedium of eternity by games of cards. But they find this impossible, because, whenever a pack is shuffled, it comes out in perfect order, beginning with the ace of spades and ending with the king of hearts. There is a special department of Hell for students of probability. In this department there are many typewriters and many monkeys. Every time a monkey walks on a typewriter, it types by chance one of Shakespeare's sonnets. . . .

There is a peculiarly painful chamber inhabited solely by philosophers who have refuted Hume. These philosophers, though in Hell, have not learned wisdom. They continue to be governed by their animal propensity toward induction. But every time that they have made an induction, the next instance falsifies it. This, however, happens only during the first hundred years of their damnation. After that, they learn to expect that an induction will be falsified, and therefore it is not falsified until another century of logical torment has altered their expectation. Throughout all eternity surprise continues, but each time at a higher logical level. (N.E.P.)

When we pass in review the opinions of former times which are now recognized as absurd, it will be found that nine times out of ten they were such as to justify the infliction of suffering. Take, for instance, medical practice. When anaesthetics were invented they were thought to be wicked as being an attempt to thwart God's will. Insanity was thought to be due to diabolic possession, and it was believed that demons inhabiting a madman could be driven out by inflicting pain upon him, and so making them uncomfortable. In pursuit of this opinion, lunatics were treated for years on end with systematic and conscientious brutality. I cannot think of any instance of an erroneous medical treatment that was agreeable rather than disagreeable to the patient. (U.E.)

The absence of any sharp line between men and apes is very awkward for theology. When did men get souls? Was the Missing Link capable of sin and therefore worthy of hell? Did Pithecanthropus Erectus have moral responsibility? Was Homo Pekiniensis damned? (I.S.S.)

A man who uses what is called 'bad language' is not from a rational point of view any worse than a man who does not. Nevertheless practically everybody in trying to imagine a saint would consider abstinence from swearing an essential. Considered in the light of reason this is simply silly. The same applies to alcohol and tobacco. With regard to alcohol the feeling does not exist in southern countries, and indeed there is an element of impiety about it, since it is known that Our Lord and the Apostles drank wine. With regard to tobacco it is easier to maintain a negative position, since all the greatest saints lived before its use was known. But here also no rational argument is possible. The view that no saint would smoke is based in the last analysis upon the view that no saint would do anything solely because it gave him pleasure. (C.H.)

When Benjamin Franklin invented the lightning-rod, the clergy, both in England and America, with enthusiastic support of George III, condemned it as an impious attempt to defeat the will of God. For, as all right-thinking people were aware, lightning is sent by God to punish impiety or some other grave sin—the virtuous are never struck by lightning. Therefore if God wants to strike anyone, Benjamin Franklin ought not to defeat His design; indeed, to do so is helping criminals to escape. But God was equal to the occasion, if we are to believe the eminent Dr Price, one of the leading divines of Boston. Lightning having been rendered ineffectual by the 'iron points invented by the sagacious Dr Franklin,' Massachusetts was shaken by earthquakes, which Dr Price perceived to be due to God's wrath at the 'iron points.' In a sermon on the subject he said, 'In Boston are more erected than elsewhere in New England, and Boston seems to be more dreadfully shaken. Oh! There is no getting out of the mighty hand of God.' Apparently, however, Providence gave up all hope of curing Boston of its wickedness, for, though the lightning-rods became more and more common, earthquakes in Massachusetts have remained rare. Nevertheless, Dr Price's point of view, or something very like it, was still held by one of the most influential men of recent times. When, at one time, there were several bad earthquakes in India, Mahatma Gandhi solemnly warned his compatriots that these disasters had been sent as a punishment for their sins. (U.E.)

There are logical difficulties in the notion of Sin. We are told that Sin consists in disobedience to God's commands, but we are also told that God is omnipotent. If He is, nothing contrary to His will can occur; therefore when the sinner disobeys His commands, He must have intended this to happen. St Augustine boldly accepts this view, and asserts that men are led to sin by a blindness with which God afflicts them. But most theologians, in modern times, have felt that, if God causes men to sin, it is not fair to send them to Hell for what they cannot help. We are told that sin consists in acting contrary to God's will. This, however, does not get rid of the difficulty. Those who, like Spinoza, take God's omnipotence seriously, deduce that there can be no such thing as sin. This leads to frightful results. Why! said Spinoza's contemporaries, was it not wicked of Nero to murder his mother? Was it not wicked of Adam to eat the apple? Is one action just as good as another? Spinoza wriggles, but does not find any satisfactory answer. *If* everything happens in accordance with God's will, God must have wanted Nero to murder his mother; therefore, since God is good, the murder must have been a good thing. From this argument there is no escape. (U.E.)

The Roman Catholic Church demands legislation such that, if a woman becomes pregnant by a syphilitic man, she must not artificially interrupt her pregnancy, but must allow a probably syphilitic child to be born, in order that, after a few years of misery on earth, it may spend eternity in limbo (assuming its parents to be non-Catholics). The British State considers it the duty of an Englishman to kill people who are not English whenever a collection of elderly gentlemen in Westminster tells him to do so. Such instances suffice to illustrate the fact that Church and State are implacable enemies of both intelligence and virtue. (E.S.O.)

Suppose we wish—as I certainly do—to find arguments against Nietzsche's ethics and politics, what arguments can we find? The question is: If Buddha and Nietzsche were confronted, could either produce an argument that ought to appeal to the impartial listener? I am not thinking of political arguments. We can imagine them appearing before the Almighty, as in the first chapter of the Book of Job, and offering advice as to the sort of world He should create. What could either say?

Buddha would open the argument by speaking of the lepers, outcast and miserable; the poor, toiling with aching limbs and barely kept alive by scanty nourishment; the wounded in battle, dying in slow agony; the orphans, ill-treated by cruel guardians; and even the most successful haunted by the thought of failure and death. From all this load of sorrow, he would say, a way of salvation must be found, and salvation can only come through love.

Nietzsche, whom only Omnipotence could restrain from interrupting, would burst out when his turn came: 'Good heavens, man, you must learn to be of rougher fibre. Why go about snivelling because trivial people suffer? Or, for that matter, because great men suffer? Trivial people suffer trivially, great men suffer greatly, they are noble. Your ideal is a purely negative one, absence of suffering, which can be completely secured by nonexistence. I, on the other hand, have positive ideals: I admire Alcibiades, and the Emperor Frederick II, and Napoleon. For the sake of such men, any misery is worth while. I appeal to You, Lord, as the greatest of creative artists, do not let Your artistic impulses be curbed by the degenerate, fear-ridden maunderings of this wretched psycopath.'

Buddha, who in the courts of Heaven has learnt all history since his death, and has mastered science with delight in knowledge and sorrow at the use to which men have put it, replies with calm urbanity: 'You are mistaken, Professor Nietzsche, in thinking my ideal a purely negative one. True, it includes a negative element, the absence of suffering; but it has in addition quite as much that is positive as is to be found in your doctrine. Though I have no special admiration for Alcibiades and Napoleon, I too have my heroes: My successor Jesus, because he told men to love their enemies; the men who discovered how to master the forces of nature and secure food with less labour; the medical men who have shown how to diminish disease; the poets and artists and musicians who have caught glimpses of the Divine beatitude. Love and knowledge and delight in beauty are not negations; they are enough to fill the lives of the great men that have ever lived.'

'All the same,' Nietzsche replies, 'your world would be insipid. You should study Heraclitus, whose works survive complete in the celestial library. Your love is compassion, which is elicited by pain; your truth. if you are honest, is pleasant, and only to be known through suffering; and as to beauty, what is more beautiful than the tiger. who owes his splendour to fierceness? No, if the Lord should decide for your world, I fear we should all die of boredom.'

'You might,' Buddha replies, 'because you love pain, and your love of life is a sham. But those who really love life would be happy as no one is happy in the world as it is.' (H.W.P.)

According to Saint Thomas, evil is unintentional, not as essence, and has an accidental cause which is good. All things tend to be like God, who is the End of all things. Human happiness does not consist in carnal pleasures, honour, glory, wealth, worldly power, or goods of the body, and is not seated in the sense. Man's ultimate happiness does not consist in acts of moral virtue, because these are means; it consists in the contemplation of God. But the knowledge of God possessed by the majority does not suffice; nor the knowledge of Him obtained by faith. In this life, we cannot see God in His essence, or have ultimate happiness; but hereafter we shall see Him face to face. (Not literally, we are warned, because God has no face.) This will happen not by our natural power, but by the divine light; and even then, we shall not see all of Him. (H.W.P.)

Those who first advocated religious toleration were thought wicked, and so were the early opponents of slavery. The Gospels tell how Christ opposed the stricter forms of the Sabbath taboo. It cannot, in view of such instances, be denied that some actions which we all think highly laudable consist in criticizing or infringing the moral code of one's own community. Of course this only applies to past ages or to foreigners; nothing of the sort could occur among ourselves, since our moral code is perfect. (H.S.E.P.)

Protestants tell us, or used to tell us, that it is contrary to the will of God to work on Sundays. But Jews say that it is on Saturdays that God objects to work. Disagreement on this point has persisted for nineteen centuries, and I know no method of putting an end to the disagreement except Hitler's lethal chambers, which would not generally be regarded as a legitimate method in scientific controversy. Jews and Mohammedans assure us that God forbids pork, but Hindus say that it is beef that he forbids. Disagreement on this point has caused hundreds of thousands to be massacred in recent years. It can hardly be said, therefore, that the Will of God gives a basis for an objective ethic. (H.S.E.P.)

I know men, by no means old, who, when in infancy they were seen touching a certain portion of their body, were told with the utmost solemnity: 'I would rather see you dead than doing that.' I regret to say that the effect in producing virtue in later life has not always been all that conventional moralists might desire. Not infrequently threats are used. It is perhaps not so common as it used to be to threaten a child with castration, but it is still thought quite proper to threaten him with insanity. Indeed, it is illegal in the State of New York to let him know that he does not run the risk unless he thinks he does. The result of this teaching is that most children in their earliest years have a profound sense of guilt and terror which is associated with sexual matters. The association of sex with guilt and fear goes so deep as to become almost or wholly unconscious. I wish it were possible to institute a statistical inquiry, among men who believe themselves emancipated from such nursery tales, as to whether they would be as ready to commit adultery during a thunderstorm as at any other time. I believe that ninety per cent of them, in their heart of hearts, would think that if they did so they would be struck by lightning. (M.M.)

The Platonic Socrates was a pattern to subsequent philosophers for many ages. What are we to think of him ethically? (I am concerned only with the man as Plato portrays him.) His merits are obvious. He is indifferent to worldly success, so devoid of fear that he remains calm and urbane and humorous to the last moment, caring more for what he believes to be truth than for anything else whatever. He has, however, some grave defects. He is dishonest and sophistical in argument, and in his private thinking he uses intellect to prove conclusions that are to him agreeable, rather than in a disinterested search for knowledge. There is something smug and unctuous about him, which reminds one of a bad type of cleric. His courage in the face of death would have been more remarkable if he had not believed that he was going to enjoy eternal bliss in the company of the gods. Unlike some of his predecessors, he was not scientific in his thinking, but was determined to prove the universe agreeable to his ethical standards. This is treachery to truth, and the worst of philosophic sins. As a man, we may believe him admitted to the communion of saints; but as a philosopher he needs a long residence in a scientific purgatory. (H.W.P.)

Since reason consists in a just adaptation of means to ends, it can only be opposed by those who think it a good thing that people should choose means which cannot realize their professed ends. This implies either that they should be deceived as to how to realize their professed ends, or that their real ends should not be those that they profess. The first is the case of a populace misled by an eloquent *fuehrer*. The second is that of the schoolmaster who enjoys torturing boys, but wishes to go on thinking himself a benevolent humanitarian. I cannot feel that either of these grounds for opposing reason is morally respectable. (H.S.E.P.)

One critic takes me to task because I say that only evil passions prevent the realization of a better world, and goes on triumphantly to ask, 'are all human emotions necessarily evil?' In the very book that leads my critic to this objection, I say that what the world needs is Christian love, or compassion. This, surely, is an emotion, and, in saying that this is what the world needs, I am not suggesting reason as a driving force. I can only suppose that this emotion, because it is neither cruel nor destructive, is not attractive to the apostles of unreason. (H.S.E.P.)

Intellectually, the effect of mistaken moral considerations upon philosophy has been to impede progress to an extraordinary extent. I do not myself believe that philosophy can either prove or disprove the truth of religious dogmas, but ever since Plato most philosophers have considered it part of their business to pro-

duce 'proofs' of immortality and the existence of God.
They have found fault with the proofs of their predecessors—Saint Thomas rejected Saint Anselm's proofs,
and Kant rejected Descartes'—but they have supplied
new ones of their own. In order to make their proofs
seem valid, they have had to falsify logic, to make
mathematics mystical, and to pretend that deep-seated
prejudices were heaven-sent intuitions. (H.W.P.)

All who are not lunatics are agreed about certain
things. That it is better to be alive than dead, better to
be adequately fed than starved, better to be free than a
slave. Many people desire those things only for themselves and their friends; they are quite content that their
enemies should suffer. These people can be refuted by
science: Mankind has become so much one family that
we cannot insure our own prosperity except by insuring
that of everyone else. If you wish to be happy yourself,
you must resign yourself to seeing others also happy.
(S.S.S.)

The Stoic-Christian view requires a conception of virtue
very different from Aristotle's, since it must hold that
virtue is as possible for the slave as for his master.
Christian ethics disapproves of pride, which Aristotle
thinks a virtue, and praises humility, which he thinks a
vice. The intellectual virtues, which Plato and Aristotle
value above all others, have to be thrust out of the list
altogether, in order that the poor and humble may be
able to be as virtuous as anyone else. Pope Gregory the
Great solemnly reproved a bishop for teaching gram-
mar. (H.W.P.)

There is no pretence of justice, as we understand it, in
the punishment following an act forbidden by a taboo,
which is rather to be conceived as analogous to death as
the result of touching a live wire. When David was
transporting the Ark on a cart, it jolted over a rough
threshing floor, and Uzzah, who was in charge, thinking
it would fall, stretched up his hand to steady it. For this
impiety, in spite of his laudable motive, he was struck
dead (II Samuel vi. 6–7). The same lack of justice

appears in the fact that not only murder, but accidental homicide, calls for purification. (H.S.E.P.)

It must be admitted that there is a certain type of Christian ethic to which Nietzsche's strictures can be justly applied. Pascal and Dostoevsky—his own illustrations—have both something abject in their virtue. Pascal sacrificed his magnificent mathematical intellect to his God, thereby attributing to Him a barbarity which was a cosmic enlargement of Pascal's morbid mental tortures. Dostoevsky would have nothing to do with 'proper pride'; he would sin in order to repent and to enjoy the luxury of confession. (H.W.P.)

Forms of morality based on taboo linger on into civilized communities to a greater extent than some people realize. Pythagoras forbade beans, and Empedocles thought it wicked to munch laurel leaves. Hindus shudder at the thought of eating beef; Mohammedans and orthodox Jews regard the flesh of the pig as unclean. St Augustine, the missionary to Britain, wrote to Pope Gregory the Great to know whether married people might come to church if they had had intercourse the previous night, and the Pope ruled that they might only do so after a ceremonial washing. There was a law in Connecticut—I believe it is formally unrepealed—making it illegal for a man to kiss his wife on Sunday. (H.S.E.P.)

It is true that if we ever did stop to think about the cosmos we might find it uncomfortable. The sun may grow cold or blow up; the earth may lose its atmosphere and become uninhabitable. Life is a brief, small, and transitory phenomenon in an obscure corner, not at all the sort of thing that one would make a fuss about if one were not personally concerned. But it is all monkish and futile—so scientific man will say—to dwell on such cold and unpractical thoughts. Let us get on with the job of fertilizing the desert, melting Arctic ice, and killing each other with perpetually improving technique. Some of our activities will do good, some harm, but all alike will show our power. And so, in this godless universe, we shall become gods. (I.S.S.)

Law in origin was merely a codification of the power of dominant groups, and did not aim at anything that to a modern man would appear to be justice. In many Germanic tribes, for example, if you committed a murder, you were fined, and the fine depended upon the social status of your victim. Wherever aristocracy existed, its members had various privileges which were not accorded to the plebs. In Japan before the Meiji era began a man who omitted to smile in the presence of a social superior could legally be killed then and there by the superior in question. This explains why European travellers find the Japanese a smiling race. (N.H.C.W.)

The Christian ethics inevitably, through the emphasis laid upon sexual virtue, did a great deal to degrade the position of women. Since the moralists were men, woman appeared as the temptress; if they had been women, man would have had this role. Since woman was the temptress, it was desirable to curtail her opportunities for leading men into temptation; consequently respectable women were more and more hedged about with restrictions, while the women who were not respectable, being regarded as sinful, were treated with the utmost contumely. It is only in quite modern times that women have regained the degree of freedom which they enjoyed in the Roman Empire. The patriarchal system did much to enslave women, but a great deal of this was undone just before the rise of Christianity. After Constantine, women's freedom was again curtailed under the pretence of protecting them from sin. It is only with the decay of the notion of sin in modern times that women have begun to regain their freedom. (M.M.)

As men begin to grow civilized, they ceased to be satisfied with mere taboos, and substitute divine commands and prohibitions. The Decalogue begins: 'God spoke these words and said.' Throughout the Books of Law it is the Lord who speaks. To do what God forbids is wicked, and will also be punished. Thus the essence of morality becomes obedience. The fundamental obedience is to the will of God, but there are many derivation forms which owe their sanction to the fact that social inequalities have been divinely instituted. Subjects must obey the king, the slaves their master, wives their husbands, and children their parents. The king owes obedience only to God, but if he fails in this he or his people will be punished. When David took a census, the Lord, who disliked statistics, sent a plague, of which many thousands of the children of Israel died (I Chron xxi). This shows how important it was for everybody that the king should be virtuous. The power of priests depended partly upon the fact that they could to some extent keep the king from sin, at any rate from the grosser sins such as worship of false gods. (H.S.E.P.)

Kant was never tired of pouring scorn on the view that the good consists of pleasure, or of anything else except virtue. And virtue consists in acting as the moral law enjoins, *because* that is what the moral law enjoins. A right action done from any other motive cannot count as virtuous. If you are kind to your brother because you are fond of him, you have no merit; but if you can hardly stand him and are nevertheless kind to him because the moral law says you should be, then you are the sort of person that Kant thinks you ought to be. But in spite of the total worthlessness of pleasure Kant thinks it unjust that the good should suffer, and on this ground alone holds that there is a future life in which they enjoy eternal bliss. If he really believed what he thinks he believes, he would not regard heaven as a place where the good are happy, but as a place where they have never-ending opportunities of doing kindnesses to people whom they dislike. (H.S.E.P.)

Kant invented a new moral argument for the existence of God, and that in varying forms was extremely popular during the nineteenth century. ... The point I am concerned with is that, if you are quite sure there is a difference between right and wrong, you are then in this situation: Is that difference due to God's fiat or is it not? If it is due to God's fiat, then for God Himself there is no difference between right and wrong, and it is no longer a significant statement to say that God is good. If you are going to say, as theologians do, that God is good, you must then say that right and wrong have some meaning which is independent of God's fiat, because God's fiats are good and not bad independently of the mere fact that He made them. If you are going to say that, you will then have to say that it is not only through God that right and wrong come into being, but that they are in their essence logically anterior to God. You could, of course, if you liked, say that there was a superior deity who gave orders to the God who made this world, or you could take up the line that some of the gnostics took up—a line which I often thought was a very plausible one—that as a matter of fact this world that we know was made by the devil at a moment when God was not looking. There is a good deal to be said for that, and I am not concerned to refute it. (W.N.C.)

To a modern mind, it is difficult to feel enthusiastic about a virtuous life if nothing is going to be achieved by it. We admire a medical man who risks his life in an epidemic of plague, because we think illness is an evil, and we hope to diminish its frequency. But if illness is no evil, the medical man might as well stay comfortably at home. To the Stoic, his virtue is an end in itself, not something that does good. And when we take a longer view, what is the ultimate outcome? A destruction of the present world by fire, and then a repetition of the whole process. Could anything be more devastatingly futile? There may be progress here and there, for a time, but in the long run there is only recurrence. When we see something unbearably painful, we hope that in time such things will cease to happen; but the Stoic assures us that what is happening now will happen over and over again. Providence, which sees the whole, must, one would think, ultimately grow weary through despair. (H.W.P.)

When I was a child the atmosphere in the house was one of puritan piety and austerity. There were family prayers at eight o'clock every morning. Although there were eight servants, food was always of Spartan simplicity, and even what there was, if it was at all nice, was considered too good for children. For instance, if there was apple tart and rice pudding, I was only allowed the rice pudding. Cold baths all the year round were insisted upon, and I had to practise the piano from seven-thirty to eight every morning although the fires were not yet lit. My grandmother never allowed herself to sit in an armchair until the evening. Alcohol and tobacco were viewed with disfavour although stern convention compelled them to serve a little wine to guests. Only virtue was prized, virtue at the expense of intellect, health, happiness, and every mundane good. (P.F.M.)

For over two thousand years it has been the custom among earnest moralists to decry happiness as something degraded and unworthy. The Stoics, for centuries, attacked Epicurus, who preached happiness; they said that his was a pig's philosophy, and showed their superior virtue by inventing scandalous lies about him. One of them, Cleanthes, wanted Aristarchus persecuted for advocating the Copernican system of astronomy; another, Marcus Aurelius, persecuted the Christians; one of the most famous of them, Seneca, abetted Nero's abominations, amassed a vast fortune, and lent money to Boadicea at such an exorbitant rate of interest that she was driven into rebellion. So much for antiquity. Skipping the next two thousand years, we come to the German professors who invented the disastrous theories that led Germany to its downfall and the rest of the world to it present perilous state; all these learned men despised happiness, as did their British imitator, Carlyle, who is never weary of telling us that we ought to eschew happiness in favour of blessedness. He found blessedness in rather odd places: Cromwell's Irish massacres, Frederick the Great's bloodthirsty perfidy, and Governor Eyre's Jamaican brutality. (P.F.M.)

Apart from logical cogency, there is to me something a little odd about the ethical valuations of those who think that an omnipotent, omniscient, and benevolent

Deity, after preparing the ground by many millions of years of lifeless nebulae, would consider Himself adequately rewarded by the final emergence of Hitler and Stalin and the H-bomb. (W.N.C.)

The persistence of personal identity which is assumed by the criminal law, and also in the converse process of awarding honours, becomes to one who has reached my age almost a not readily credible paradox. A prudent man imbued with the scientific spirit will not claim that his present beliefs are wholly true, though he may console himself with the thought that his earlier beliefs were perhaps not wholly false. (B.W.B.R.)

I think only cruel people could have invented hell. People with humane feelings would not have liked the thought that those who do things on earth which are condemned by the morality of their tribe will suffer eternally without any chance of amendment. I do not think decent people would have ever adopted that view. (B.R.S.M.)

Our own morality is full of taboos. There are all sorts, even in the most august things. Now there is one sin definitely recognized to be a sin, which I have never committed. It says, 'Thou shalt not covet thy neighbour's Ox.' Now I never have. (B.R.S.M.)

Sometimes in a vision I see a world of happy human beings, all vigorous, all intelligent, none of them oppressing, none of them oppressed. A world of human beings aware that their common interests outweigh those in which they compete, striving towards those really splendid possibilities that the human intellect and the human imagination make possible. Mankind is all one family and we can all be happy or we can all be miserable. The time is passed when you could have a happy minority living upon the misery of the great mass. That is passed forever. People will not acquiesce in it and you have to learn to put up with your neighbour's happiness. (B.R.S.M.)

I think it is very likely that *Joan of Arc* believed she was a witch. A great many people condemned as witches did believe they were witches, and there was an enormous spread of cruelty. Now Sir Thomas Browne, you would say when you read his works, seems like a very humane and cultivated person; but he actually took part in trials of witches on the side of persecution, and he said that to deny witchcraft is a form of atheism, because after all the Bible says, 'Thou shalt not suffer a witch to live.' Therefore, in elementary logic, if you do not think it is right to burn them—if you think they are witches, you must be disbelieving in the Bible and therefore be an atheist. (B.R.S.M.)

A fanatical group all together have a comfortable feeling that they are all friends with one another. They are all very much excited about the same thing. You can see it in any closed party. There is always a fringe of fanatics in any closed group and they feel very cosy with one another and when that is spread about and is combined with a propensity to hate some other group you get fanaticism well developed. You hate the people who do not share your fanaticism. (B.R.S.M.)

I think ethical taboos have been bad because it was held important that people should believe something for which there did not exist good evidence and that falsified everybody's thinking, falsified systems of education, and set up also, I think, complete moral heresy; namely, that it is right to believe certain things, and wrong to believe certain others, apart from the question of whether they are true or false. In the main, I think that ethical taboos have done a great deal of harm largely by sanctifying conservatism and adhesion to ancient habits, and still more by sanctifying intolerance and hatred. (B.R.S.M.)

The police both in the east and the west have a curious belief that if you studied the opposite system you would infallibly agree with it, and therefore we must not be allowed to know anything about it. This view is really absurd. People may be unjustly suspected and completely ruined but for some classified reason this kind of morality is not open to question by either side. (B.R.S.M.)

I had a very pleasant time in jail. But ordinarily it is very difficult for a man accustomed to mental work. It is easier if you are accustomed to manual work, because you are not deprived of so much of your mental life. If I had been sentenced for stealing spoons I should have felt that I had been deservedly disgraced. (B.R.S.M.)

You should look into whether sexual morality does any harm or not. I should deal with sexual morality as I should with everything else. I should say that if what you are doing does no harm to anybody there is no reason to condemn it. But some earnest moralists warn us that this is a mistake. (B.R.S.M.)

Drug sellers tell me that if I took their drugs my hair would turn black again. I am not sure that I should like that, because the whiter my hair becomes the more ready people are to believe what I say, but nobody should be *certain* of everything. The business of a philosopher is to understand the world and if people solve their social problems *Religion* will die out. (B.R.S.M.)

Human nature is infinitely malleable and that is what people do not realize. Now if you compare a domestic dog with a wild wolf you will see what training can do. The domestic dog is a nice comfortable creature, barks occasionally, and he may bite the postman, but on the whole he is all right; whereas the wolf is quite a different thing. Now you can do exactly the same thing with human beings. Human beings according to how they are treated will turn out totally different and I think the idea that you cannot change human nature is so silly. (B.R.S.M.)

Civilized states spend more than half their revenue on killing each other's citizens. Consider the long history of the activities inspired by moral fervour: human sacrifices, persecutions of heretics, witch-hunts, pogroms leading up to wholesale extermination by poison gases. Are these abominations, and the ethical doctrines by which they are prompted, really evidence of an intelligent Creator? And in all high seriousness can we really wish that the men who practised them should live forever? The world in which we live can be understood as a result of muddle and the accidental collocations of atoms; but if it is the outcome of deliberate purpose, the purpose must have been that of a fiend. For my part, I find accident a less painful and more plausible hypothesis. (w.N.C.)

Three passions, simple but overwhelmingly strong, have governed my life: the longing for love, the search for knowledge, and unbearable pity for the suffering of mankind. These passions, like great winds, have blown me hither and thither, in a wayward course, over a deep ocean of anguish, reaching to the very verge of despair.

I have sought love, first, because it brings ecstasy— ecstasy so great that I would often have sacrificed all the rest of life for a few hours of that joy. I have sought it, next, because it relieved loneliness—that terrible loneliness in which one shivering consciousness looks over the rim of the world into the cold unfathomable lifeless abyss. I have sought it, finally, because in the union of love I have seen, in a mystic miniature, the prefiguring vision of the heaven that saints and poets have imagined. This is what I sought, and though it might seem too good for human life, this is what—at last—I have found. (a.B.R. Vol. I.)

I may have thought the road to a world of free and happy human beings shorter than it is proving to be, but I was not wrong in thinking that such a world is possible, and that it is worth while to live with a view to bringing it nearer. I have lived in the pursuit of a vision, both personal and social. Personal: to care for what is noble, for what is beautiful, for what is gentle; to allow moments of insight to give wisdom at more mundane times. Social: to see in imagination the society that is to be created, where individuals grow freely, and where hate and greed and envy die because there is nothing to nourish them. These things I believe, and the world, for all its horrors, has left me unshaken. (A.B.R. Volume III, Postscript.)

Epilogue

IT is difficult to begin any book and it is even harder to end it. But when any specific side of the work of an eminent man is involved, the editor is caught in an unusual predicament; to say too much is expected, to say too little is unforgiveable. Voltaire was misrepresented until the twentieth century when a few brave admirers had the courage to pay tribute to his august wit. In his day the world was expected to be a neat, orderly place to live in. Voltaire thought otherwise, and mused at the phony elegance of his time, and laughed at the incompetence of his contemporaries. Lord Russell mused at the harsh realities of a world immersed in scientific discoveries that left no room for laughter. However, mere fun on the surface was not entirely what Lord Russell had in mind. Nevertheless, each advance in science diminishes the chance that there will be any fun to be had anywhere in the future.

Acknowledgements

THE editor will always be grateful to Lord Russell for having spent some of his valuable time in correcting, with his own hand, the first draft of this volume before it was originally published in 1958. Nor will the editor forget the kindness of Lord and Lady Russell in approving the final draft. Nor will the editor forget Lord Russell's kindness in writing a special Preface for this new revised edition shortly before his death.

Sixteen years is a long time and in this new edition there will appear many additional extracts from all the major works of Lord Russell since 1956. In every case the purpose is to illustrate his unique gift for satire— not satire for satire's sake, but rather for the purpose of inviting intelligent inspection of the value of centuries of cherished myths. This book reflects Lord Russell's final message to humanity, but not in solemn cadences.

The editor wishes to express a special thanks to his wife, Margaret Wilson Egner, for her kindness as this book grew. Without her help this book would not have been possible. The editor also wishes to thank the following persons for their generous suggestions in the preparation of this anthology: Professor Alvan J. Obelsky, Karen Sandstrom, Gladys Lober, Marvin O. Hunt, Milton S. Wilson, Anne Sherrill, Dick Egner, Delores Reed, and Beatrice Garza, for typing the manuscript.

The editor reserves a final thanks to Sir Stanley Unwin and Rayner Unwin for their kindness over the years.

For arrangements made with various publishers whereby certain copyrighted material was permitted to be reprinted, and for the courtesy extended by them, the following acknowledgements are gratefully made:

George Allen & Unwin Ltd. and Simon and Schuster: for permission to use excerpts from Lord Russell's:

A History of Western Philosophy	(1945)
New Hopes for a Changing World	(1951)
Unpopular Essays	(1950)
Impact of Science on Society	(1953)
Nightmares of Eminent Persons	(1955)
Authority and the Individual	(1949)
Satan in the Suburbs	(1953)
Human Society in Ethics and Politics	(1954)
Portraits from Memory	(1956)
Why I Am Not a Christian	(1957)

George Allen & Unwin Ltd. and W. W. Norton and Company, Inc.: for permission to quote material from Lord Russell's:

Power: A New Social Analysis	(1938)
Education and the Social Order (English title)	(1932)
Education and the Modern World (American title)	
An Outline of Philosophy (English title)	(1927)
Philosophy (American title)	

Beacon Press: for permission to reprint excerpts from:

'The Political and Cultural Influence,' in *The Impact of America on European Culture*
(1951)

George Allen & Unwin Ltd. and Liveright Publishing Corporation: for permission to use excerpts from Lord Russell's:

Marriage and Morals   (1929)
The Conquest of Happiness   (1930)

The Oxford University Press, London and New York: for permission to use excerpts from Lord Russell's:

Religion and Science   (1935)

LOOK MAGAZINE: for permission to use excerpts from Lord Russell's article:

'What Is an Agnostic' in the November 3, 1953, issue.

COMMON SENSE: for permission to reprint excerpts from Lord Russell's:

'Why Radicals Are Unpopular'
                              (March 1936)

NEW YORK TIMES MAGAZINE: for permission to quote material from two articles by Lord Russell:

'To Face Danger Without Hysteria'
                              (January 21, 1951)
'The Science to Save us from Science'
                              (March 19, 1950)

UNITED NATIONS WORLD: for permission to reprint excerpts from Lord Russell's article:

'Boredom or Doom in a Scientific World'
                              (September 1948)

Robert Egner

Robert Egner is currently Professor of Philosophy at Shelby State Community College in Memphis, Tennessee. In addition to this volume, Professor Egner is the author of ART AND MUSIC IN THE HUMANITIES, and is the editor of THE BASIC WRITINGS OF BERTRAND RUSSELL.

BERTRAND RUSSELL'S BEST has been translated into French, Spanish, Italian, Swedish, Chinese and Japanese. "If there is a continuing demand for this book," said Russell in a letter to Professor Egner dated September 25, 1969, "it is a tribute to the understanding and care that you have shown in its preparation. I hope that we may give pleasure and provoke independent thought."

WAR AND FOREIGN POLICY

(0451)

☐ **THE WORLD AT WAR by Mark Arnold-Forster.** Here are the battles, the generals, the statesmen, the heroes, and the fateful decisions that shaped the vast, globe-encircling drama that was World War II. You saw this thrilling epic on TV. Now it comes to life on the printed page more vividly and comprehensively than it ever has before. (127331—$3.95)

☐ **STRATEGY by B. H. Liddell Hart.** Taking all of world military history as its subject and World War II as its focal point, this classic book examines wars and their architects. Now, for the first time, we can truly understand why Hitler almost won—and ultimately lost—World War II.
(143264—$4.95)†

☐ **THE AMERICAN STYLE OF FOREIGN POLICY by Robert Dallek.** In the past century, American foreign policy has played an increasingly dominant role in world events. Yet all too often, according to the author of this ground-breaking book, this policy has been a reflection of American internal concerns rather than a response to international realities. "Engaging"—*The New Republic* (622960—$4.50)*

☐ **RUSSIA AND THE WEST UNDER LENIN AND STALIN by George F. Kennan.** Ambassador Kennan's historical perspective of Soviet-Western relations is full and authentic; it covers the period from the Bolshevik uprising to the cold war; it deals with such figures of destiny as Wilson, Lenin, Curzon, Stalin, Molotov, Hitler, and Roosevelt. "Surely one of the most important books since the end of the last war..."—Edmund Wilson.
(624602—$4.95)*

† Not available in Canada
*Prices slightly higher in Canada